To

Fernando!

Be Happy –

    Be Healthy –

        Be Well!

Laura Theodore

EASY VEGAN
HOME COOKING

EASY VEGAN
HOME COOKING

OVER 125 PLANT-BASED AND GLUTEN-FREE RECIPES
FOR WHOLESOME FAMILY MEALS

LAURA THEODORE

HOST OF *JAZZY VEGETARIAN* ON NATIONAL PUBLIC TELEVISION

*My constant quest is to support
and help make the world
a kinder, more compassionate, and
healthier home for all living beings.
I dedicate this book to all of the animals.
They are the voiceless, and I pray
that my voice may speak for them.*

—LAURA THEODORE

Chicken-ish Salad
(page 56)

CONTENTS

INTRODUCTION
Easy Meals *At* Home

AROUND THE WORLD, more of us are *staying* at home and *cooking* at home. Whether you are an accomplished vegan chef or just learning the craft of creating pleasing home-cooked meals for your family, it has become increasingly essential to find accessible, nutritious, and delicious recipes that feature simple staples and plant-powered pantry ingredients, making it doable for serving delicious, easy-to-prepare vegan menus at home.

With many people seeking a healthier diet and turning to fruits, vegetables, grains, nuts, seeds, and legumes for meal preparation, I decided it was time to share some appealing, easy, and nourishing plant-based recipes—each using a *limited number* of readily available ingredients, with most requiring minimal prep time.

All of the mouth-watering recipes in this book are vegan *and* gluten-free, suitable for serving any day of the week, and require only *eight ingredients or fewer* (non-inclusive of water, salt, black pepper, and olive oil), focusing on bountiful breakfasts, light lunches, satisfying suppers, celebratory meals, and delightful desserts—all designed to please vegans, vegetarians, and omnivores—adults and kiddos alike!

This new normal finds many of us challenged to produce three meals a day to suit a family with varied tastes. Creating quick, tasty meals in our own home kitchen requires utilizing convenient pantry staples, combined with refrigerated and frozen

items. In this inspired book, I take away the guess work by sharing pantry "must-haves," how to stock a vegan refrigerator and freezer, quick cooking tips, easy flavor enhancers, and effective plant-based substitutions. Preparation and cooking times are also included with each recipe.

Every lip-smacking chapter features 100% plant-powered, gluten-free recipes for *Easy Vegan Home Cooking!* It is my hope that this comprehensive volume of yummy dishes will help make your life a little bit easier, less stressful, healthier and—oh yes, totally *jazzylicious*!

Now, let's get started!

COOKING THE EASY VEGAN WAY!

I STRONGLY BELIEVE THAT eating "animal-free" is healthier for us, the planet and, of course, the animals. The easier it is to cook plant-based meals at home, the more people will adopt a vegan diet. Having the proper basic food items stocked in your kitchen makes it easier to prepare home cooked meals to please your family. In this chapter I have listed some of my best time-saving tips, lists, and ideas for preparing quick, tasty and healthy vegan meals.

So, what makes a vegan recipe *easy*?

- **Easy-to-find ingredients.** Often, plant-based recipes call for specialized foods that may be challenging to purchase at the supermarket, so it's important to have vegan recipes on hand that utilize accessible ingredients. That is why all of the recipes in this book incorporate ingredients that can be found at any well-stocked supermarket.
- **Easy-to-follow instructions.** Even though some of the fancier recipes in this book have extra steps, they all have simple-to-follow instructions that make them doable for family meals, even if you're just starting out on the path to cooking plant-based menus.
- **Easy to "please the palate."** Many of the recipes in this book are centered around classic dishes based on my family's recipes or traditional American favorites. When it's a breeze to please your family by serving vegan dishes they savor and appreciate, it makes cooking easier!

- **Easy clean-up.** Care was taken when creating these recipes to minimize ingredients, bowls, pots, pans, and utensils necessary to prepare each dish, achieving quicker preparation *and* faster clean up! Plus, each of the recipes in this book use eight ingredients or fewer (non-inclusive of water, salt, black pepper, and olive oil), making it quicker to gather ingredients for each recipe, while requiring less time to put them away after each recipe is prepared.

PLANT-BASED "MUST-HAVES"

Over the past several years, I have found that I depend more and more on pantry staples and frozen foods for getting quick, delicious, and nutritious vegan meals on the table. Having the right pantry items or frozen ingredients on hand makes the journey toward preparing mindful, plant-powered meals less daunting and *easier* to please the varied palates of my family.

STOCKING THE PANTRY

Keeping a well-stocked cupboard, while emphasizing a well-planned variety of items is crucial for creating easy meals at home. Below, I list my top essentials for creating easy and delicious meals at home.

LAURA'S EASY PANTRY PICKS
Canned Beans

I like to keep a wide variety of canned beans in my pantry like black, kidney, white, pinto, and garbanzo beans. Canned beans add convenience to your weekly menu plan and make a great base for creating hearty, nutrient-dense, protein rich, and fiber filled vegan meals. Beans are inexpensive and extremely versatile. I use canned beans for vegan burgers, burritos, soups, casseroles, salads, meatless loaves, plant-based "cheese," vegan "cream" sauces, appetizers, dips, and so much more. I like to purchase organic beans packed in cans made with BPA-free lining. Make certain to refrigerate canned beans after opening.

Marinara Sauce and Canned Tomatoes

A good, jarred, organic vegan marinara is my *go-to* staple for creating easy, satisfying weeknight meals, making a time-saving base for pasta dishes, lasagna, chili, sauces, casseroles, stews, soups, and more. I keep several varieties stocked in my pantry for use when time is at a premium. Canned (BPA-free) tomatoes provide the same flexibility for creating easy meals. I keep organic diced, crushed, *and* fire-roasted canned tomato varieties on hand. Make certain to refrigerate marinara sauce and/or canned tomatoes after opening.

Dairy-Free Milk

I store a wide variety of aseptic packed dairy-free milk in my pantry. Plus, I keep several *refrigerated* types on hand, too. Soy, almond, rice, oat, macadamia, cashew, coconut, hemp, and hazelnut dairy-free milks are now readily available in both non-refrigerated (aseptic) packaging and in the refrigerated section of well-stocked supermarkets. These plant-based milks make the perfect substitute for dairy milk in recipes for baked goods, breakfast cereals, smoothies, vegan ice "cream," casseroles, mashed potatoes, and so much more. Make certain to refrigerate aseptic packed dairy-free milk after opening.

Rolled Oats

I keep gluten-free, quick cooking and/or old fashioned rolled oats in my pantry. Rolled oats are yummy in so many recipes, and they're really versatile, too! I use rolled oats in cookies, muffins, pie crusts, cakes, crisps, pie fillings, quick breads, meatless loafs, gravies, and vegan burgers. For a hearty breakfast, I like oatmeal cooked with dairy-free milk (in place of water), raisins, and unsweetened shredded dried coconut, served with maple syrup and more dairy-free milk on the side. Plus, in less than 5-minutes, you can turn rolled oats into fresh flour! To make quick, homemade oat flour, simply pour some rolled oats into a blender and process into coarse or fine flour. (See full instructions for making oat flour on page 27.) I recommend refrigerating rolled oats after opening.

NOTE: *Old fashioned rolled oats* are whole oats that are steamed and rolled into flat flakes. *Quick cooking rolled oats* are made with the same process, but the flat flakes are cut into smaller pieces allowing for a shorter cooking time. Most of the recipes

in this book that require rolled oats use *quick cooking rolled oats.* If you only have *old fashioned rolled oats* in your pantry when preparing one of the *quick cooking rolled oats* recipes in this book, simply put the old fashioned oats into a blender or food processor and pulse a few times to break down the oats just *slightly.* Proceed with the recipe as directed.

Quinoa

White or tri-color quinoa is another staple I like to store in my pantry. With a welcoming nutty taste and packed with plenty of high quality, plant-based protein, quinoa is often touted as being a super food and makes an excellent alternative to brown rice. Quinoa is technically a seed (not a grain), but its texture, taste, and preparation method echoes that of many whole-grains, so it is often categorized as a grain. I use quinoa as a main dish (cooked with canned beans or peas), side dish, or as a base for quick plant-based burgers, casseroles, meatless loaves, and salads. I recommend refrigerating quinoa after opening.

Tahini

Tahini is made by grinding hulled (or unhulled) sesame seeds into a creamy paste. Tahini is traditionally used in hummus, but I use it in cookies, pie crusts, salad dressings, smoothies, vegan burgers, meatless loaves and more. Tahini is available in jars or cans and is found in the nut butter or ethnic food section of well-stocked supermarkets. Make certain to refrigerate tahini after opening.

MORE PANTRY STABLE ITEMS FOR EASY MEALS

Here's a basic list of additional essential ingredients that I keep stocked in my pantry.

- Baby artichoke hearts (canned, packed in water, refrigerate after opening)
- Cereal (ready to eat, unsweetened, several varieties)
- Coconut (unsweetened dried, shredded and/or flaked)
- Extra-virgin olive oil (store at room temperature after opening)
- Ketchup (refrigerate after opening)
- Lentils (dry, red, French, green, and/or brown varieties)
- Mushrooms (canned, organic, sliced cremini and/or white button, refrigerate after opening)
- Mustard (Dijon and/or spicy brown, refrigerate after opening)
- Nuts (raw and roasted cashews, pecans, and walnuts, refrigerate after opening, or freeze for long-term storage)
- Olives (jarred and canned, pimento stuffed Spanish-style Manzanilla, black, and Kalamata varieties, refrigerate after opening)
- Pineapple (canned chunks and crushed in 100% juice, refrigerate after opening)
- Raisins, dried cherries, and sweetened, dried cranberries
- Rice (organic brown short-grain, long-grain, and basmati, refrigerate after opening)
- Salsa (mild, medium and/or hot, refrigerate after opening)
- Sriracha-style hot sauce (refrigerate after opening)
- Soup (canned, BPA free, vegan, several varieties)
- Sunflower seeds (roasted and salted and/or raw, refrigerate after opening)
- Sweeteners (vegan dark brown sugar, vegan cane sugar, and maple syrup)
- Tamari *or* coconut aminos (gluten-free, refrigerate after opening)
- Tofu (gluten-free aseptic cartons, several varieties, refrigerate after opening) See *Easy Tofu Tips* (page 10). Note: I keep refrigerated tubs of tofu stocked, too. See *Stocking the Refrigerator* (page 7).
- Vegetable broth (aseptic cartons) and/or vegan, gluten-free bouillon cubes (refrigerate after opening)

Easy Green Beans with Vegan Butter Sauce (page 202)

STOCKING THE FREEZER

These days, I increasingly depend upon my freezer to have frozen items stored when fresh food is not on hand. Having frozen produce like; green veggies for casseroles, fruits for smoothies, veggie burgers for quick meals, and a few other goodies ensures that I can put together easy meals that are tasty and nutritious.

Here's a short list of frozen foods I like to keep in the freezer:

- Bananas (peeled and frozen in tightly sealed freezer bags)
- Blueberries, strawberries and/or raspberries
- Broccoli (florets)
- Burgers (vegan, gluten-free)
- Green beans

- Mangoes (sliced or cubed)
- Peaches (sliced)
- Peas
- Pineapple (canned chunks, drained well and frozen for *up to a week* in tightly sealed freezer bags)

STOCKING THE REFRIGERATOR

Here's a list of the basic produce used in this book, along with a few other essentials that are best kept in your refrigerator. These items are sold in the refrigerated and/or produce sections of your supermarket.

- Apples
- Asparagus
- Avocado
- Bananas
- Bell peppers (orange, yellow, red, and/or green)
- Blueberries
- Broccoli
- Cabbage
- Carrots
- Cauliflower
- Celery
- Cucumber
- Dairy-free milk (refrigerated varieties like soy, almond, oat, macadamia, rice, cashew, and/or coconut)
- Dates (Medjool are preferred)
- Eggplant
- Green beans
- Kale (curly, red, or *lacinato* "dinosaur kale")

- Lemons *and* limes
- Lettuce (romaine, leafy green, and/or spring green mix)
- Mushrooms (cremini, white button, and Portobello)
- Onions* (purple or red, sweet, and yellow)
- Potatoes** (white, russet, red, and baby varieties)
- Scallions and/or chives
- Spinach (baby)
- Squash (acorn, butternut, summer, Delicata, and zucchini)
- Strawberries
- Sweet potatoes and/or yams
- Tempeh (plain, 3-grain, and/or 5-grain)
- Tofu (gluten-free, *extra-firm* and *super-firm* regular tofu, in refrigerated tubs)
- Tomatoes (plum, cherry, grape, and/or "slicing" varieties)

* Store onions away from potatoes, or onions may be stored in a cool, well-ventilated, dark place, if preferred.

** Store potatoes away from onions, or potatoes may be stored in a cool, well-ventilated, dark place, if preferred.

STOCKING THE SPICE RACK

Cooking with dried herbs and spices is an easy way to add flavor to plant-based recipes. I love incorporating dried herbs and spices into my daily meals and desserts. In this book, I have made it easier to season many of the recipes using herb and spice *blends.* When I want to give recipes a big burst of flavor in an instant, I reach for *one* jar of seasoning *blend* instead of opening *six or seven* jars of herbs and/or spices! It's less time-consuming and saves time when you're in a hurry to get a yummy vegan meal on the table!

Here's my essential list of herb and spice blends, along with my short list of single dried herbs and spices used in this book. I highly recommend that you keep the following stocked in your spice cabinet.

Essential Herb and Spice Blends

- All-purpose seasoning blend
- Chili powder
- Curry powder
- Garam masala
- Italian seasoning blend (use your favorite variety or see recipe on page 112)
- Pumpkin pie spice

Single Herbs and Spices

- Black and rainbow pepper (whole peppercorns, in grinder)
- Cayenne pepper
- Cinnamon (ground)
- Crushed red pepper flakes
- Garlic powder
- Paprika (smoked *and* sweet)
- Sea salt and/or Himalayan pink salt
- Turmeric (ground)

EASY EGG SUBSTITUTIONS

Vegan baking without the use of eggs can be challenging! When converting conventional baked goods recipes into vegan versions, a certain amount of experimentation is often needed—but here, I've saved you the time. Here are four of my quick and easy vegan egg substitutions.

- **For an effective, basic binding agent**, add 1 small mashed ripe banana to your recipe to replace each egg for a dense and sweet baked goodie.
- **To add structure *and* binding**, replace each egg with 1 tablespoon freshly ground flaxseeds mixed with 3 tablespoons water *or* add 1 tablespoon freshly ground flaxseeds to your *dry* ingredients, then add an extra 3 to 4 tablespoons of dairy-free milk, juice, or water when incorporating your *wet* ingredients into the batter.
- **For leavening baked goods without eggs**, mix 1 to 1¼ cups dairy-free milk with 2 to 3 tablespoons lemon juice and let stand for 5 to 10 minutes. This will produce vegan "buttermilk." Then, add a bit of baking soda to the batter. The baking soda will react to the acidic base in the vegan "buttermilk," helping your baked goods to rise beautifully!
- **When converting a conventional recipe that calls for only one egg**, in most cases that one egg can be omitted and the recipe will still yield a successful result!

EASY VEGAN CREAM SAUCES

Making a vegan cream sauce is so simple! There are many easy, plant-based combinations that provide a rich tasting sauce for every dietary need. Here are three of my favorites:

- **Cauliflower "cream" sauce** provides a low-fat vegan cream sauce option. Cut a head of cauliflower into florets and steam until tender. Cool slightly. Put the cooled, steamed cauliflower in a blender container and process with a bit of unsweetened dairy-free milk until smooth, adding more dairy-free milk as needed to achieve desired consistency.
- **Cashew "cream" sauce** is a favorite of mine. To make this creamy sauce, soak raw cashews in the refrigerator with just enough water to cover, for 1 to 4 hours, then drain and rinse the cashews well. Put the soaked cashews in a blender container and process with a bit of water until smooth, adding more water as needed to achieve desired consistency.
- **White Bean "cream" sauce** is a lower-in-fat, protein-packed, cream sauce option. Drain and rinse 1 can of white beans (any variety) then put the beans in a blender container and process with a bit of unsweetened dairy-free milk until smooth, adding more dairy-free milk as needed to achieve desired consistency.

EASY TOFU TIPS

Tofu is high in plant-protein and it can enhance just about any plant-based meal. Tofu (alone) has a somewhat bland taste, making it essential to add flavorings and/or seasonings to it in order to transform the tofu into a delicious, versatile ingredient.

Tofu adds a welcome texture to many vegan dishes. It is wonderful baked, sautéed, steamed, fried, breaded, roasted, whipped, cubed, and/or mashed and it can function as a satisfying base for any course of a meal, from festive appetizers to hearty main dishes to creamy desserts!

Types of Tofu

Tofu is made from soybeans, water, and coagulant. It is widely available in supermarkets. Plain tofu comes in two main forms: regular (packed in water and refrigerated in plastic wrapping or tubs) and silken (packed in both aseptic cartons and refrigerated tubs). Each type of tofu is available in soft, firm, and extra-firm varieties. *Super*-firm regular tofu is now widely available, too.

- **Silken tofu** (available in refrigerated tubs or aseptic packaging): Silken tofu does not hold its shape well, so it is ideal to use in creamy and/or blended recipes like smoothies, desserts, puddings, salad dressings, sauces, and dips.

- **Firm and extra-firm regular tofu** (available in refrigerated tubs, aseptic packaging, or pre-cubed in refrigerated tubs): This type of tofu absorbs flavors well and generally holds its shape well, without pressing. When pressed, *firm* and/or *extra-firm regular tofu* will hold its shape for making tofu cutlets or "steaks." (See instructions for "How to Press Tofu" on the following page.) Both *firm* and/or *extra-firm regular tofu* are excellent choices for slicing, cubing, mashing, and/or using in creamy desserts that need extra structure. This type of tofu can be sautéed or baked and it is excellent when mashed up with additional flavorings to use in a tofu scramble, vegan "ricotta cheese," or eggless salad.

- **Super-firm tofu** (generally available in plastic wrapped refrigerated blocks): This pre-pressed, ready to cube (or slice) tofu is *extremely* firm, making it ideal to incorporate into many dishes in place of meat. It holds its shape flawlessly and is perfect for slicing into "cutlets" or cutting into cubes. Note: Super-firm tofu is *very* dense, so it is not recommended to use in "creamy" or "mashed" tofu recipes.

How to Cut Tofu

When preparing firm, extra-firm, or super-firm tofu, start by taking the tofu out of its packaging and putting it into a colander that has been placed in the sink. Using clean hands or a rubber spatula, *gently* press down on the block of tofu to drain some of the excess water out of it. Put the lightly drained block of tofu on a cutting board then cut it into slices or cubes. (Alternately, you may press the tofu before cutting, see below.)

For uniform slices or "cutlets," cut the block of tofu in half *widthwise*, then cut each half into 4 to 8 slices, depending upon the thickness desired. For cubes, cut the tofu into thirds *lengthwise* to make 3 identical slabs. Stack the slabs on top of each other and slice through them twice, *lengthwise* (again) to make 9 even "columns," then slice several times across the stacked "columns," to make 1- to 1½-inch cubes of tofu.

How to Press Tofu

For some recipes requiring baking or sautéing with *firm* and/or *extra-firm regular tofu* (refrigerated tubs), it is important to press the excess liquid out of the tofu first, so that your recipe does not become too watery. If you cook with tofu often, I highly recommend purchasing a tofu press. However, if you do not own a tofu press, you may press the tofu by putting the block of tofu on a rimmed dinner plate that has been covered in a layer of paper towels or clean kitchen towel. Put another layer of towels on top of the tofu. Put another plate (or a small cutting board) on top of the paper towels and weigh it down with a heavy object (like a few soup cans). Refrigerate; after 1 to 3 hours, drain the water that has been pressed out of the tofu. Your tofu is now ready for use in any recipe requiring pressed tofu.

EASY COOKING TIPS

Here are several basic techniques that I like to use in order to make preparing family meals easier.

- To save time, I often wash my salad greens in advance of preparing dinner. To do so, wash and then spin your salad greens dry, then place them in a large bowl. Place a dry paper towel on top of the greens, cover the bowl, and chill. Your greens will be super crisp and ready to toss into your salad at suppertime.

- Frozen bananas make a tasty base for making quick smoothies or frozen desserts. First, peel several ripe bananas and cut them into thick slices. Put the slices into a freezer bag, tightly seal and freeze. When dessert time comes around, (for each serving) put 1 large, sliced frozen banana, 1 tablespoon maple syrup, and ⅓ to ½ cup vanilla or chocolate flavored dairy-free milk into the blender. Blend until creamy, adding more dairy-free milk as needed. Tastes just like soft serve and the kiddos love it!

- OK…I'll admit it. When I am short on time, I sometimes use *canned* mushroom slices, making an excellent time-saver when preparing sauces, casseroles, stews, or soups. I drain the mushroom slices *thoroughly* before using them and proceed! Here are a few recipes in this book that use canned mushrooms: *Pantry Polenta Lasagna* (page 123) and *Eggplant Lasagna with Vegan Chive Ricotta* (page 129).

- I like to pre-bake extra russet, yellow, and/or sweet potatoes to be used in various recipes throughout the week. Cold, cooked potatoes make a wonderful base for an eggless veggie scramble, casserole, or vegetable sauté. For quick oven fries, slice several cold, baked potatoes into thick wedges, toss with olive oil, salt, and pepper and roast at 400°F for 40 to 50 minutes, until golden and crispy. In this book, I have used pre-cooked potatoes in *Easy Twice-Baked Spuds* (page 182).

- When I cook rice or quinoa, I often make a double batch to use in recipes later in the week. Pre-cooked rice or quinoa are excellent choices to add to casseroles, soups, stir-fries, or salads. For a hearty breakfast treat, try heating up cooked rice or quinoa along with some dairy-free milk and a splash of maple syrup. Yum! In this book I have used cooked quinoa in *Festive Stuffed Peppers* (page 166), *Minty Quinoa Salad* (page 51), *Quinoa and Curly Parsley Bowl* (page 52), and *Big Protein Quinoa Casserole* (page 116).

*Pantry Polenta
Lasagna
(page 123)*

- To decrease the fat content in many savory dishes, you can replace some or all of the oil used in stovetop cooking with vegetable broth or water. Use 3 tablespoons of either veggie broth or water to replace 1 tablespoon of oil. Unlike oil, these liquids will evaporate during cooking, so be very watchful and add more as needed.

SALT AND PEPPER—MADE EASY!

I love adding salt and pepper to most savory recipes, but many of us have varied tastes or dietary requirements when it comes to these two popular seasonings. It is for that reason that *exact* amounts of salt and pepper are not included in many of the recipes in this book. If a recipe requires a *precise* amount of salt and/or pepper to make it taste optimal, the exact amount is included in the ingredients list. If the inclusion of either salt or pepper is only a matter of choice, I have left it up to you to season to taste, as desired.

TABLE OF EQUIVALENT MEASURES

This is a must-have list for any home cook. Use this handy chart for easily doubling or tripling recipes, adapting pre-existing recipes, or cutting a recipe in half.

THIS:	EQUALS THIS:
3 teaspoons	1 tablespoon
4 tablespoons	¼ cup
5 tablespoons plus 1 teaspoon	⅓ cup
8 tablespoons	½ cup
12 tablespoons	¾ cup
16 tablespoons	1 cup (or 8 ounces)
2 cups	1 pint (or 16 ounces)
4 cups	1 quart (or 32 ounces)
4 quarts	1 gallon (or 128 ounces)

EASY RECIPES!

All of the recipes in this cookbook are 100% vegan, require a minimal amount of ingredients, and are designed to help you easily incorporate delicious, plant-based meals into your weekly menu plan. These recipes were created to please omnivores, vegetarians, and long-time vegans alike, and are suitable for beginner cooks, too.

So what are we waiting for? Let's get to the recipes!

*Blueberry-Coconut
Coffee Cake
(page 26)*

THE RECIPES

Oatmeal, Date & Ap,
Breakfast Crisp
(page 24)

BREAKFAST & QUICK-BAKED GOODIES

Whether you prefer an early day meal or like to wait until mid-morning for your first bite of the day, these tempting recipes will surely satisfy. From tasty breakfast grains and quick-baked muffins, to a yummy eggless scramble and refreshing smoothie—these top o' the morning treats will keep you going until lunchtime!

QUINOA PORRIDGE
WITH CINNAMON AND RAISINS

Makes 3 to 4 servings ■ **Prep Time:** 5 minutes / **Stove Top:** 16 to 18 minutes

Quinoa is often thought of as a supper side dish, but it makes perfect break-fast fare, too. It's rich in fiber and high-quality protein to start your day in a hearty way.

2¼ cups water

1 cup uncooked quinoa, rinsed thoroughly

2 to 3 tablespoons raisins

¼ teaspoon ground cinnamon, plus more for serving

1 tablespoon vegan buttery spread (optional)

Dairy-free milk, for serving

1 tablespoon maple syrup, for serving

Put the water, quinoa, raisins, and cinnamon in a medium-sized saucepan and bring to a boil over medium heat. Decrease the heat to low, cover, and simmer for 16 to 18 minutes, until the water is absorbed and the quinoa is very soft. Remove from the heat and stir in the optional vegan buttery spread, if desired. Cover and let stand 5 minutes.

Spoon the quinoa into cereal bowls and sprinkle with more cinnamon. Serve hot, with dairy-free milk and maple syrup, on the side.

PUMPKIN PIE BREAKFAST RICE

Makes 3 to 4 servings ■ **Prep Time:** 5 minutes / **Stove Top:** 40 to 45 minutes

In place of oatmeal, my mom often served white rice left over from dinner, transforming it into a yummy, hot breakfast cereal. This recipe is my jazzed up version of a childhood favorite.

2¼ cups water

1 cup brown basmati rice, rinsed

2 to 3 tablespoons raisins or sweetened dried cranberries

¼ teaspoon salt

¼ teaspoon pumpkin pie spice (use ½ teaspoon for spicier rice)

Dairy-free milk, for serving

Maple syrup, for serving

Put the water, rice, raisins (or cranberries), salt, and pumpkin pie spice into a medium-sized saucepan and bring to a boil over medium-high heat. Decrease the heat to medium-low, cover, and simmer for 40 to 45 minutes, or until the water is absorbed and the rice is *very* soft and tender. Cover and let stand for 10 minutes. Spoon the rice into cereal bowls. Serve hot, with dairy-free milk and maple syrup on the side.

SAVORY ASPARAGUS TOFU SCRAMBLE

Makes 4 servings ▪ **Prep Time:** 15 minutes / **Stove Top:** 15 to 20 minutes

This delightful scramble makes a satisfying breakfast, brunch, or luncheon entrée. The lemon adds pizzazz without overpowering the dish. Serve with sliced fruit and muffins on the side for a hearty, early day meal.

1 medium yellow or sweet onion, diced

1 tablespoon plus 1 teaspoon extra-virgin olive oil, divided

2 teaspoons gluten-free tamari *or* coconut aminos

1 small bunch fresh asparagus, tough ends removed and cut into 1- to 2-inch pieces

1 tablespoon water, plus more as needed

1 block (15 to 16 ounces) extra-firm regular tofu (refrigerated tub), drained

¾ tablespoon freshly squeezed lemon juice

¼ teaspoon ground turmeric

⅛ teaspoon salt

Freshly ground black pepper, to taste

½ cup shredded vegan cheese (optional)

Put the onion, 1 tablespoon olive oil, and tamari in a large skillet. Cover and cook over medium-low heat for 5 to 7 minutes or until the onion is slightly soft, adding 1 tablespoon water, as needed, if the pan becomes dry. Add the asparagus, adding a bit more water as needed, 1 tablespoon at a time. Cover and cook for about 3 minutes or until the asparagus is *just* crisp tender.

While the onion and asparagus cook, put the tofu, lemon juice, turmeric, salt, black pepper, and 1 teaspoon olive oil in a medium-sized bowl. Mash together using a potato masher or large fork, until the tofu resembles the consistency of scrambled eggs. Add the tofu mixture to the skillet, and gently fold it into the onion and asparagus. Cover, and let cook over medium-low heat, for 4 to 5 minutes, or until the underside of the tofu mixture begins to turn slightly golden. Sprinkle the top of the tofu with the optional vegan cheese. Cover and let cook for 1 minute. Stir the mixture together (to incorporate the vegan cheese), cover and let cook for 2 to 4 minutes or until the tofu is heated through and becomes slightly golden. Serve warm.

OATMEAL, DATE & APPLE BREAKFAST CRISP

Makes 4 servings ■ **Prep Time:** 10 minutes / **Bake Time:** 40 to 43 minutes

A cross between a crisp and a crumble, this sweet and fruity casserole can be served for a festive breakfast or healthy dessert.

FRUIT LAYER

1 teaspoon extra-virgin olive oil (to lightly coat baking dish)

3 cups cored and cubed apples (1- to 1½-inch cubes, leave peels on)

½ cup pitted and diced dates

¼ cup sweetened dried cranberries

2 tablespoons maple syrup

1 teaspoon ground cinnamon

PECAN-OAT TOPPING

1½ cups gluten-free, quick cooking rolled oats

1 cup chopped pecans

½ cup shredded unsweetened dried coconut

8 tablespoons maple syrup, divided

2 tablespoons extra-virgin olive oil (see Chef's Note), plus more as needed

1 teaspoon ground cinnamon

Preheat the oven to 400°F. Lightly coat a 10½- x 7½-inch (or similarly sized) baking dish with 1 teaspoon olive oil.

FRUIT LAYER

To make the fruit layer, put the apples, dates, cranberries, 2 tablespoons maple syrup, and 1 teaspoon ground cinnamon into a medium-sized bowl and stir with a large spoon to combine. Transfer the apple mixture to the prepared baking dish and spread it in an even layer.

PECAN-OAT TOPPING

To make the pecan-oat topping, put the oats, pecans, coconut, 6 tablespoons maple syrup, 2 tablespoons olive oil, and 1 teaspoon ground cinnamon into a medium-sized bowl and stir with a large spoon to thoroughly combine. Spread the oat/pecan mixture over the apples in an even layer.

Cover and bake for 25 minutes. Uncover and bake for an additional 10 minutes. Drizzle 2 tablespoons maple syrup over the top of the crisp and bake for another 5 to 8 minutes, or until the topping is slightly golden. Transfer the casserole to a wire rack and let cool for 5 minutes before serving. Spoon into shallow bowls and serve with dairy-free milk on the side, if desired. Tightly covered and stored in the refrigerator, the crisp will keep for 2 days.

■ If preferred, you can use vegan buttery spread in place of the olive oil.

BLUEBERRY-COCONUT COFFEE CAKE
WITH CINNAMON STREUSEL TOPPING

Makes 6 to 8 servings ■ **Prep Time:** 22 minutes / **Bake Time:** 55 to 65 minutes

This sweet and fruity, coconut-laced cake makes an excellent choice for a mid-morning coffee break or delightful dessert.

¼ cup plus 3 tablespoons extra-virgin olive oil, divided, plus more for coating pan

2½ cups freshly ground, gluten-free oat flour, divided (see box on the next page)

1 cup unsweetened shredded dried coconut

1¼ cups vegan cane sugar, divided

2 teaspoons baking powder

2½ teaspoons ground cinnamon, divided

1¼ cups unsweetened dairy-free milk

1¼ cups fresh blueberries

Preheat the oven to 350°F. Generously coat a 9-inch round cake pan with olive oil.

Put 2 cups oat flour into a large bowl. Add the shredded coconut, ¾ cup sugar, baking powder, and 1 teaspoon cinnamon and stir with a dry whisk to combine.

Make a well in the center of the dry ingredients and add the dairy-free milk and ¼ cup olive oil. Stir with a large spoon to combine. Fold in the blueberries. Transfer the batter to the prepared cake pan.

To make the streusel topping, put ½ cup oat flour, ½ cup sugar, and 1½ teaspoons ground cinnamon into a small bowl and stir with a dry whisk to combine. Add 3 tablespoons olive oil and stir with a dough blender (or your clean hands) until the mixture resembles wet sand. Distribute the streusel evenly over the top of the batter.

Bake for 55 to 65 minutes, or until the top of the cake is golden and a toothpick inserted into the center of the cake comes out clean. Transfer the pan to a wire rack and gently run a table knife around the perimeter of the cake. Let cool for at least 30 minutes before slicing and serving. (If the cake is warm, it will still be quite soft.) Stored tightly covered in the refrigerator, leftover cake will keep for about 2 days.

How to Make Oat Flour

To make freshly ground, gluten-free oat flour, put rolled oats into a blender (or food processor) and process into coarse (or fine) flour.

3 cups gluten-free, quick cooking (or gluten-free, old fashioned) rolled oats will yield approximately 2½ cups oat flour.

3¼–3½ cups gluten-free, quick cooking (or gluten-free, old fashioned) rolled oats will yield approximately 2¾ cups oat flour.

If desired, you may use pre-packaged, milled gluten-free oat flour for any recipe in this book that calls for freshly ground oat flour. However, freshly ground oat flour is preferable and will create a lighter baked goodie!

BREAKFAST OATMEAL CAKE BAKE

Makes 6 servings ■ **Prep Time:** 20 minutes / **Bake Time:** 48 to 52 minutes

Part oatmeal, part cake, this tempting treat makes a substantial top-of-the day offering. Bonus: It serves as a mid-morning companion for a coffee (or tea) break, and it makes an excellent afternoon snack, too!

⅓ cup extra-virgin olive oil, plus more for coating pan

3 tablespoons golden flaxseeds

2⅓ cups freshly ground, gluten-free oat flour (see "How to Make Oat Flour," page 27)

1½ teaspoons baking powder

¼ teaspoon salt

⅔ cup (*very* firmly packed) vegan dark brown sugar

⅔ cup unsweetened shredded dried coconut

1 cup unsweetened *or* sweetened dairy-free milk

½ cup water

2¼ cups cored and chopped red apples (any variety, do not peel first)

⅓ cup raisins

½ teaspoon ground cinnamon (optional)

Preheat the oven to 375°F. Line the bottom of an 8-inch square, rimmed baking pan with unbleached parchment paper, leaving an overhang of 2-inch "wings" on two sides of the pan. Lightly oil the other two sides of the pan.

Put the flaxseeds in a high-performance blending appliance and process into fine flour. Put the flaxseed flour into a large bowl. Add the oat flour, baking powder, and salt and stir with a dry whisk to combine. Add the brown sugar and coconut and stir with the whisk to incorporate.

Make a well in the center of the dry ingredients and add the dairy-free milk, ⅓ cup olive oil, and water and stir with a large spoon to combine. Fold in the apples and raisins.

Pour the batter into the prepared pan and sprinkle the optional cinnamon over the top. Bake for 48 to 52 minutes, or until the edges of the cake are golden and a toothpick inserted into the center of the cake comes out *almost* clean. Transfer the pan to a wire rack and let cool for 10 minutes. Cake will be soft when warm.

Lift the cake out of the pan using the paper "wings," and put it on the wire rack. Let cool for an additional 10 to 20 minutes, cut into squares, and serve. Stored in an airtight container in the refrigerator, the cake will keep for about 3 days.

JUMBO PEANUT BUTTER-BANANA BREAKFAST COOKIES

Makes 12 cookies ■ **Prep Time:** 20 minutes / **Bake Time:** 20 to 25 minutes

These satisfying cookies make festive, fun, and satisfying breakfast fare. Oh, yes—they function as a healthful snack or delicious dessert, too!

2½ cups gluten-free, quick cooking rolled oats

½ teaspoon baking powder

½ teaspoon baking soda

1 scant cup lightly mashed ripe bananas (about 1½ large bananas or 2 medium-sized bananas)

⅓ cup smooth peanut butter

¼ cup maple syrup

¼ cup raisins (see Chef's Note)

¼ cup vegan dark chocolate chips (see Chef's Note)

Preheat the oven to 350°F. Line a large, rimmed baking sheet with unbleached parchment paper.

Put the oats, baking powder, and baking soda into a large bowl and stir with a dry whisk until combined.

Put the bananas, peanut butter, and maple syrup into a medium-sized bowl and stir with a large spoon until combined, leaving some chunky bits of banana. Add the banana mixture to the oat mixture and stir to combine. (The dough will be quite stiff and thick.) Fold in the raisins and chocolate chips.

Drop about 3 tablespoons of the cookie dough onto the prepared sheet and flatten slightly with a rubber spatula. Continue in this manner with the remaining dough. Bake for 20 to 25 minutes, or until the edges are golden brown and cookies are almost set. Transfer the cookies to a wire rack and let cool for 8 to 15 minutes. Stored in an airtight container in the refrigerator, cookies will keep for about 3 days.

CHEF'S NOTE

■ You may use *just* raisins or *just* chocolate chips in this recipe, if desired.

COCO-NUTTY APPLE MUFFINS

Makes 18 muffins ■ **Prep Time:** 20 minutes / **Bake Time:** 30 to 35 minutes

Apples, walnuts, and coconut make an enticing trio to add appeal to these tasty, moist, and sweet breakfast, brunch, or snack muffins.

3 cups gluten-free, quick cooking rolled oats, divided

½ cup plus 3 tablespoons unsweetened shredded dried coconut

1 cup plus 2¼ teaspoons vegan cane sugar, divided

2 teaspoons baking powder

¼ teaspoon salt

1½ cups cored and diced apples, with peel (sweet, red apple varieties are best)

1 cup chopped walnuts

1½ cups plain sweetened *or* unsweetened dairy-free milk

⅓ cup extra-virgin olive oil

Preheat the oven to 350°F. Line a 12-cup standard muffin tin and a 6-cup muffin tin with paper liners.

Put 2 cups rolled oats into a blender (or food processor) and process into fine flour.

Put the oat flour, remaining 1 cup rolled oats, coconut, 1 cup sugar, baking powder, and salt into a large bowl and stir with a dry whisk until combined. Add the apples and walnuts and stir to combine.

Make a well in the center of the dry ingredients. Add the dairy-free milk and olive oil, and stir with a large spoon to combine.

Divide the batter evenly among the 18 muffin cups. Sprinkle ⅛ teaspoon of vegan cane sugar over the top of each muffin.

Bake for 30 to 35 minutes, or until a toothpick inserted into the center of a muffin comes out clean.

Put the muffin tins on a wire rack and let cool for 30 minutes. Serve warm, at room temperature or cold. Covered tightly and stored in the refrigerator, leftover muffins will keep for about 3 days.

PIÑA COLADA MUFFINS

Makes 18 muffins ■ **Prep Time:** 12 minutes / **Bake Time:** 32 to 38 minutes

Shredded coconut and crushed pineapple add texture and flavor to these oh-so-delicious, super moist, but not-too-sweet snack muffins.

2¼ cups plus 3 tablespoons (firmly packed) pre-packaged *or* freshly ground gluten-free oat flour, plus more if needed (see "How to Make Oat Flour," page 27)

¾ cup plus 2¼ teaspoons vegan cane sugar, divided

2 teaspoons baking powder

¼ teaspoon salt

½ cup plus 2 tablespoons unsweetened shredded dried coconut

1 can (14 ounces) unsweetened crushed pineapple, with juice (see Chef's Note)

1 cup sweetened dairy-free milk

1 cup chopped pecans

Preheat the oven to 375°F. Line a 12-cup standard muffin tin and a 6-cup muffin tin with paper liners.

Put the flour, ¾ cup sugar, baking powder, and salt into a large bowl and stir with a dry whisk until combined. Add the pecans and coconut and stir to combine.

Make a well in the center of the dry ingredients. Add the crushed pineapple (with juice) and the dairy-free milk and stir with a large spoon to combine. If the batter still seems too "wet," add 1 more tablespoon of oat flour.

Divide the batter evenly among the 18 muffin cups. Sprinkle the top of each muffin with about ⅛ teaspoon sugar. Bake for 32 to 38 minutes, or until a toothpick inserted into the center of a muffin comes out clean.

Put the muffin tins on a wire rack and let cool for 30 minutes. Serve warm, at room temperature or cold. Covered tightly and stored in the refrigerator, leftover muffins will keep for about 3 days.

CHEF'S NOTE

■ If your can of pineapple is *more* than 14 ounces, measure out 1¾ cups of the crushed pineapple *with* juice, and then proceed with recipe as directed.

BANANA & MAPLE-WALNUT MUFFINS

Makes 18 muffins ■ **Prep Time:** 18 minutes / **Bake Time:** 25 to 30 minutes

Sweet, ripe bananas replace the eggs, and maple syrup substitutes for processed sugar in these moist and delectable "anytime" muffins!

2¾ cups (firmly packed) freshly ground, gluten-free oat flour (see "How to Make Oat Flour," page 27)

2½ teaspoons baking powder

2 teaspoons ground cinnamon

¼ teaspoon salt

2¾ cups peeled and thinly sliced ripe bananas (about 3½ to 4 large bananas)

⅔ cup maple syrup

½ cup unsweetened dairy-free milk

⅓ cup extra-virgin olive oil

1 cup chopped walnuts

Preheat the oven to 375°F. Line a 12-cup standard muffin tin and 6-cup standard muffin tin with paper liners.

Put the flour, baking powder, cinnamon, and salt into a large bowl and stir with a dry whisk to combine.

Put the bananas and maple syrup into a medium-sized bowl and mash into a very chunky purée using a potato masher or large fork, making certain that small chunks of banana are still visible.

Make a well in the center of the dry ingredients and add the banana/maple mixture, dairy-free milk, and olive oil and stir with a large spoon until thoroughly combined. Fold in the walnuts.

Divide the batter evenly among the 18 muffin cups. Bake for 25 to 30 minutes or until a toothpick inserted into the center of a muffin comes out clean.

Put the muffin tin on a wire rack and let cool at least 20 minutes before serving. Serve warm or at room temperature. Covered tightly and stored in the refrigerator, leftover muffins will keep for about 3 days.

VEGAN BUTTERMILK CORNBREAD

Makes 8 to 10 servings ■ **Prep Time:** 20 minutes / **Bake Time:** 30 to 40 minutes

Vegan "buttermilk" adds a tangy flavor to this slightly sweet cornbread. With a classic crumbly texture, this quick bread is easy-to-prepare and easier to eat. Serve it for breakfast in place of traditional toast or muffins, or pair it with your favorite soup, stew, or chili.

¼ cup plus 1 teaspoon extra-virgin olive oil, divided

1¼ cups unsweetened dairy-free milk

2 tablespoons freshly squeezed lemon juice

1¼ cups medium grind gluten-free cornmeal (see Chef's Note)

1¼ cups (firmly packed) freshly ground, gluten-free oat flour, plus more as needed (see "How to Make Oat Flour," page 27)

⅓ cup (*very* firmly packed) vegan dark brown sugar

1 tablespoon baking powder

¼ rounded teaspoon salt

Preheat the oven to 375°F. Lightly coat a 9-inch round or square cake pan with 1 teaspoon olive oil.

To make the vegan "buttermilk" put the dairy-free milk and lemon juice into a small bowl. Stir and let stand for 5 to 10 minutes, while preparing the dry ingredients.

Put the cornmeal, flour, sugar, baking powder, and salt into a large bowl and stir with a dry whisk to combine. Pour in the dairy-free milk/lemon juice mixture and ¼ cup olive oil and stir together using a large spoon until combined. Add 2 to 3 more tablespoons of oat flour if batter seems too loose (see Chef's Note). Batter should be the consistency of cake batter, but will be a bit lumpy.

Pour the batter into the prepared pan. Bake for 30 to 40 minutes, or until a toothpick inserted in the center of the cornbread comes out clean.

Put the pan on a wire rack and gently run a table knife around the perimeter of the cornbread. Cool for 20 to 30 minutes before slicing and serving. Cornbread will be crumbly. Covered tightly and stored in the refrigerator, leftover cornbread will keep for about 3 days.

CHEF'S NOTES

■ More flour may be needed depending upon how coarse (or fine) your oat flour has been ground.

■ If you are cooking gluten-free, be certain to buy certified gluten-free cornmeal to ensure that the cornmeal is completely free of gluten.

LAURA'S BLUEBERRY-BANANA SMOOTHIE

Makes 1 serving ■ **Prep Time:** 5 minutes

Frosty and fabulous, this refreshing sip features frozen ripe bananas, blueberries, and tangy tahini whirled in the blender to make a nutritious good morning beverage.

1 cup sweetened
   or unsweetened
   dairy-free milk (your
   favorite variety)

1 very large peeled, sliced,
   and frozen ripe banana

1 cup frozen blueberries
   (see Variations)

1 heaping tablespoon
   sesame tahini

Put all of the ingredients into a high-performance blending appliance. Process until smooth and creamy and serve.

VARIATIONS

■ **Laura's Peach-Banana Smoothie:** Substitute the blueberries with 1 to 1½ cups frozen sliced peaches.

■ **Laura's Pineapple-Banana Smoothie:** Substitute the blueberries with 1 to 1½ cups frozen pineapple chunks.

Confetti Potato Salad
(page 44)

SIMPLE & SATISFYING SALADS

Salads are ideal to serve as a luncheon entrée, side dish, light supper, or nutritious afternoon nosh. Here, I provide a festive array of tantalizing recipes to showcase your daily raw veggies. Potato salads, bean salads, grain bowls, green dishes, fruity choices, and snazzy toppers are all mainstays for creating easy, fresh salads for any meal of the day.

CONFETTI POTATO SALAD

Makes 8 servings ■ **Prep Time:** 50 minutes / **Refrigeration Time:** 2 to 4 hours

Colorful and quintessentially classic, this spud-based salad is easy-to-prepare and a breeze to serve. With sweet pepper rings, baby potatoes, crunchy celery, and tangy olives, it's a delicious twist on a family favorite.

8 cups cubed red or white baby potatoes, cut in half if large, leave peels on

1¾ cups mini sweet pepper rings (remove seeds and thinly slice before measuring)

1¼ cups diced celery, with leaves

½ cup minced green olives, with pimento

⅔ cup vegan mayonnaise or *Quick Vegan Mayonnaise* (page 108)

3 rounded tablespoons spicy brown or Dijon mustard

1 rounded teaspoon smoked paprika, plus more for garnish

¼ teaspoon salt

Several grinds of black pepper

Fit a steamer basket into a large pot with a tight-fitting lid. Add 2 to 3 inches of cold water, and then add the baby potatoes. Steam the potatoes for 16 to 20 minutes or until they are fork tender. Spread the potatoes in a single layer on a large, rimmed baking sheet and let cool for 15 minutes. Cover and refrigerate the potatoes for at least 30 minutes before assembling the salad (see Chef's Note).

To assemble the salad, put the potatoes, pepper rings, celery, and olives into a large bowl and stir with a large spoon to combine.

To make the dressing, put the vegan mayonnaise, mustard, paprika, and salt in a small bowl and briskly whisk to combine. Pour the dressing over the potato mixture and stir to combine. Add several grinds of black pepper, to taste, and stir to combine.

Transfer the salad to a pretty serving bowl and sprinkle with more smoked paprika. Cover and refrigerate for 2 to 4 hours before serving.

CHEF'S NOTE

■ If preferred, you may steam, cool, and refrigerate the potatoes up to 24 hours before preparing this recipe.

ARTICHOKE, OLIVE & POTATO SALAD

Makes 4 to 6 servings ▪ **Prep Time:** 50 minutes / **Refrigeration Time:** 2 to 4 hours

A creamy turmeric spiced dressing, paired with tender baby potatoes, earthy artichoke hearts, and tangy olives, combined with a few crunchy veggies makes an inviting main dish salad for a summer meal.

1½ pounds Dutch, Klondike or yellow baby potatoes, cut in half or thirds

1¾ cups diced celery, with leaves

1 can (14 to 15 ounces) water-packed artichoke hearts, drained and chopped

1 cup pitted black or Kalamata olives, chopped

2 medium carrots, grated (peeling is optional)

Sweet and Spicy Dressing (page 90) or your preferred bottled dressing

¼ teaspoon Italian seasoning blend

¼ teaspoon smoked *or* sweet paprika

Several grinds of black pepper, to taste

Fit a steamer basket into a large pot with a tight-fitting lid. Add 2 to 3 inches of cold water, and then add the baby potatoes. Steam the potatoes for 16 to 20 minutes or until they are fork tender. Spread the potatoes in a single layer on a large, rimmed baking sheet and let cool for about 30 minutes.

To assemble the salad, put the potatoes, celery, artichokes, olives, and carrots into a large bowl and stir with a large spoon to combine. Pour the *Sweet and Spicy Dressing* over the potato mixture and gently stir to combine. Sprinkle the Italian seasoning, paprika, and black pepper over the top of the salad. Cover and refrigerate for 2 to 4 hours and serve.

CHEF'S NOTE

▪ If preferred, you may steam, cool, and refrigerate the potatoes up to 24 hours before preparing this recipe.

CHICKPEA & ARTICHOKE SALAD

Makes 4 to 6 servings ■ **Prep Time:** 20 minutes / **Refrigeration Time:** 2 to 3 hours

This is a delicious and filling salad to serve as a substantial main course or hearty side dish. The chickpeas and artichoke hearts provide substance, while the spinach and sweet peppers add color and crunch. It's such a beautiful dish to look at, too! Serve this pretty salad for lunch or a light supper.

1 can (14 to 15 ounces) chickpeas (garbanzo beans), drained and rinsed

2 to 3 ounces baby spinach, finely chopped

6 sweet mini peppers (or 1 medium sweet red or orange bell pepper), seeded and thinly sliced

1 can (14 to 15 ounces) water-packed baby artichoke hearts, drained and chopped

2 tablespoons extra-virgin olive oil

2 tablespoons maple syrup

2 tablespoons good-quality balsamic vinegar *or* freshly squeezed lemon juice

⅛ teaspoon smoked paprika (optional)

⅛ teaspoon garlic powder

Salt, to taste

Freshly ground black pepper, to taste

Put the chickpeas, spinach, mini pepper slices, artichoke hearts, olive oil, maple syrup, vinegar (or lemon juice), optional paprika, and garlic powder into a large bowl. Gently stir together with a large spoon to thoroughly combine. Taste, and add salt and pepper, as desired.

Cover and refrigerate for 2 to 3 hours to allow the flavors to develop. Divide between four to six bowls and serve.

MINTY QUINOA SALAD

Makes 4 servings ▪ **Prep Time:** 20 minutes / **Refrigeration Time:** 2 to 4 hours

This refreshing mint-infused salad makes a hearty entrée for a mid-day meal or light supper. The quinoa and chickpeas provide quality plant protein, while the carrots and tomatoes impart a colorful presentation.

2½ cups cooked quinoa,
   or *Laura's Easy Quinoa*
   (page 194), well-chilled

1 cup peeled, seeded, and
   diced cucumber

1 can (14 to 16 ounces)
   chickpeas (garbanzo
   beans), drained
   and rinsed

1 cup diced fresh tomatoes

¾ cup grated or shredded
   carrots (peeling is
   optional)

2 tablespoons minced
   fresh mint

Maple-Lime Dressing (page
   94), or your preferred
   bottled dressing

Salt, to taste

Freshly ground black
   pepper, to taste

Put the cold quinoa, cucumber, chickpeas, tomatoes, carrots, and mint in a large bowl and gently stir using a large spoon, to combine.

Pour the *Maple-Lime Dressing* over the salad and gently toss until combined. Taste and add salt and pepper, to taste, if desired. Cover and refrigerate for 2 to 4 hours, to allow the flavors to develop. Serve cold.

QUINOA & CURLY PARSLEY BOWL

Makes 4 servings ■ **Prep Time:** 20 minutes / **Refrigeration Time:** 2 to 4 hours

Walnuts, roasted peppers, and olives all add punch to this filling and protein-powered quinoa based salad.

3 cups cooked quinoa, or
Laura's Easy Quinoa
(page 194), well-chilled

1 cup (firmly packed)
minced fresh
curly parsley

1 cup pitted black or
Kalamata olives, diced

1 cup walnut
halves, chopped

¾ cup thinly sliced celery

½ cup (jarred) diced roasted
red peppers

Lemon-Shallot Dressing
(page 95) or
your preferred
bottled dressing

Salt, to taste

Freshly ground black
pepper, to taste

Put the cold quinoa, parsley, olives, walnuts, celery, and red peppers in a large bowl and gently stir using a large spoon, to combine.

Pour the *Lemon-Shallot Dressing* over the salad and gently toss until combined. Taste and add salt and pepper, to taste, if desired. Cover and refrigerate for 2 to 4 hours, to allow the flavors to develop. Serve cold.

SMOKIN' COLESLAW

Makes 4 to 6 servings ■ **Prep Time:** 20 minutes / **Refrigeration Time:** 1 to 6 hours

Smokin' Coleslaw makes a great summer salad, side dish or burger topper.

5 to 5½ cups white
    and/or red cabbage,
    thinly sliced

1 cup shredded carrots
    (peeling is optional)

⅓ cup vegan mayonnaise
    or *Quick Vegan
    Mayonnaise* (page 108),
    plus more as needed

1 heaping tablespoon Dijon
    mustard, plus more
    as needed

½ teaspoon maple syrup

½ rounded teaspoon
    smoked paprika

¼ teaspoon garlic powder

⅛ teaspoon
    cayenne pepper

¼ rounded teaspoon salt,
    plus more to taste

Freshly ground black
    pepper, to taste

Put the cabbage and carrots into a large bowl.

To make the dressing, put the vegan mayonnaise, Dijon mustard, maple syrup, smoked paprika, garlic powder, cayenne pepper, and salt into a small bowl. Briskly whisk until smooth.

Pour the dressing over the cabbage mixture, and stir with a large spoon until well combined. Taste and add more mayonnaise or mustard, if desired. Add more salt and freshly ground pepper, to taste, if desired. Cover and refrigerate for at least 1 hour, or up to 6 hours, before serving.

VARIATION

■ **Smokin' Italian Coleslaw:** Add 1 rounded teaspoon *Italian seasoning blend* to the dressing. Proceed with recipe as directed.

CHICKEN-ISH SALAD

Makes 4 servings ■ **Prep Time:** 15 minutes / **Refrigeration Time:** 2 hours (optional)

Nutritious chickpeas combined with chopped artichoke hearts present a unique salad that's reminiscent of a coveted childhood classic.

SALAD

1 can (14 to 16 ounces) chickpeas (garbanzo beans), drained and rinsed

1 can (14 ounces) water-packed artichoke hearts, drained and diced

1 cup diced celery (with leaves)

¼ cup minced sweet onion

DRESSING

4 heaping tablespoons vegan mayonnaise or *Quick Vegan Mayonnaise* (page 108)

2 tablespoons spicy brown or Dijon mustard

½ teaspoon smoked paprika, plus more for garnish

¼ teaspoon salt, plus more as needed

Several grinds of black pepper, to taste

SALAD

Put all of the salad ingredients into a medium-sized bowl and stir with a large spoon to combine.

DRESSING

Put all of the dressing ingredients into a small bowl and briskly whisk to combine. Pour the dressing over the chickpea mixture and stir with a large spoon to combine.

Transfer to a pretty serving bowl and generously sprinkle with more smoked paprika, salt, and black pepper, to taste. Serve at room temperature, or cover and refrigerate for 2 hours and serve cold.

SIMPLE SUPPER SALAD

Makes 4 servings ■ **Prep Time:** 15 minutes

This colorful salad makes an easy first course for supper, but it's substantial enough to stand front and center for a light lunch served with a cup of soup and/or freshly baked muffins on the side.

SALAD

8 to 12 large leaves romaine lettuce, chopped

1½ to 2 cups thinly sliced red cabbage

2 medium tomatoes, sliced and cut into "half-moons"

8 pimento stuffed queen green olives, quartered

4 to 6 tablespoons chopped walnuts

DRESSING

3 tablespoons extra-virgin olive oil

1½ tablespoons good-quality balsamic vinegar

1½ tablespoons maple syrup

1½ tablespoons Dijon mustard

SALAD

Put the lettuce and red cabbage into a medium-sized bowl and lightly toss with tongs to combine.

Divide the lettuce/red cabbage mixture into four salad bowls or plates. Tuck one-quarter of the tomato slices slightly under the lettuce, arranging it in a pleasing manner around the perimeter of each salad. Top each salad with one-quarter of the olives and one-quarter of the walnuts. Decorate the center of each salad with a small slice of the tomato.

DRESSING

Put all of the dressing ingredients into a small bowl and briskly whisk to emulsify. Drizzle about one-quarter of the dressing over each salad and serve.

CRANBERRY, CARROT & CLEMENTINE SALAD

Makes 3 servings ■ **Prep Time:** 15 minutes / **Refrigeration Time:** 30 minutes to 24 hours

This lively combo of carrots and fruit makes a colorful first course salad or tasty side dish.

2⅔ cups grated or shredded carrots (peeling is optional)

¼ cup sweetened dried cranberries

¼ cup finely chopped walnuts

2 tablespoons vegan mayonnaise or *Quick Vegan Mayonnaise* (page 108)

2 teaspoons maple syrup

Pinch (about 1/16 teaspoon) cayenne pepper

3 clementines, tangerines, or oranges, peeled, seeded, and divided into sections.

Salt, to taste

Freshly ground black pepper, to taste

Put the carrots, cranberries, and walnuts in a medium-sized bowl and stir with a large spoon to combine.

To make the dressing, put the mayonnaise, maple syrup, and cayenne pepper into a small bowl and stir to combine. Pour the dressing over the carrot mixture and gently stir to combine. Fold in the clementine, tangerine, or orange sections. Add salt and pepper, to taste, if desired.

Cover and refrigerate for at least 30 minutes before serving (see Chef's Note). Serve cold.

CHEF'S NOTE

■ This salad holds well in the refrigerator and may be prepared up to 24 hours before serving.

GARBANZO SPINACH SALAD

Makes 2 to 4 servings ■ **Prep Time:** 10 minutes / **Refrigeration Time:** 2 hours

This fresh tasting and very substantial salad is a breeze to put together, making it a great pick for a light summer lunch.

2 cups lightly packed, finely chopped baby spinach

1 can (14 to 16 ounces) chickpeas (garbanzo beans), drained and rinsed

¼ teaspoon salt, plus more as needed, divided

1 tablespoon extra-virgin olive oil

Juice from 1 small lemon

1 small clove garlic, finely minced

Pinch (about ⅟₁₆ teaspoon) cayenne pepper

Put the spinach, chickpeas, and ⅛ teaspoon salt into a medium-sized bowl and stir to combine.

Put the olive oil, lemon juice, garlic, ⅛ teaspoon salt, and cayenne pepper in a small bowl and briskly whisk to combine. Pour the dressing over the spinach/chickpea mixture and gently toss to coat.

Cover and refrigerate for at least 2 hours or overnight before serving. Serve as a hearty side dish or light luncheon entree.

SRIRACHA-LIME GUACAMOLE

Makes 2 to 4 servings ▪ **Prep Time:** 10 minutes

A generous dash of hot sauce and chili powder provides a piquant dip. Serve with crudités for a snazzy side, lively appetizer, or light luncheon entrée.

2 medium-large ripe avocados, peeled and pitted

2 tablespoons vegan mayonnaise or *Quick Vegan Mayonnaise* (page 108)

Juice from 1 small lime (about 1½ to 2 tablespoons)

½ teaspoon sriracha-style hot sauce

½ teaspoon chili powder, plus more for garnish

⅛ teaspoon salt

Put the avocados, vegan mayonnaise, lime juice, hot sauce, chili powder, and salt into a medium-sized bowl and mash to a chunky consistency using a potato masher or large fork.

For a satisfying lunch or hearty snack, divide the guacamole between two to four dinner-sized plates and surround with carrot and celery sticks, baby artichokes, sliced tomatoes, and black or Kalamata olives. Garnish with chili powder and serve.

COCONUT-Y MAPLE "BACON" BITS

Makes ⅔ cup ■ **Prep Time:** 7 minutes / **Bake Time:** 4 to 5 minutes

These sweet, savory, and crispy little bites remind me of a certain bacon salad add-on that my mom served when I was a child. This vegan version adds piz-zazz to your daily greens by providing the perfect crunch to your salad. They are yummy to snack on, too!

⅔ cup unsweetened dried flaked coconut

1½ tablespoons maple syrup

1½ teaspoons gluten-free tamari *or* coconut aminos

1 teaspoon smoked paprika

Preheat the oven to 425°F. Line a medium-sized, rimmed baking sheet with unbleached parchment paper.

Put all of the ingredients into a medium-sized bowl and stir until thoroughly combined. Spread the coconut mixture in an even layer on the prepared pan.

Bake for 4 to 5 minutes, or until very golden brown around the edges, checking every minute, and stirring once or twice during baking. Some of the coconut pieces still will be soft, but they will crisp up a bit once cooled.

Put the pan on a wire rack and let cool 15 minutes to cool and crisp up. Store leftover "bacon" bits tightly covered in the refrigerator for up to 1 week.

TEMPTING TEMPEH "CROUTONS"

Makes 4 servings ■ **Prep Time:** 10 minutes / **Refrigeration Time:** 1 to 2 hours / **Bake Time:** 55 to 65 minutes

These dainty little tempeh bites are a great way to garnish a green salad, accompany steamed veggies, or serve atop cooked quinoa, millet, or rice.

---

1 block (8 ounces) tempeh, cut into ½- to 1-inch cubes

1 tablespoon extra-virgin olive oil

1 tablespoon maple syrup

1½ tablespoons water

½ teaspoon sriracha-style hot sauce

½ teaspoon smoked paprika

Put all of the ingredients into a medium-sized bowl and gently stir with a large spoon to combine. Cover and refrigerate for 1 to 2 hours.

Preheat the oven to 400°F. Line an 8-inch square rimmed baking pan with unbleached parchment paper. Transfer the tempeh mixture to the prepared pan and arrange it in an even layer. Cover and bake for 30 minutes.

Increase the oven temperature to 425°F. Uncover the tempeh and continue to bake for 25 to 35 minutes or until the edges are becoming very golden brown. Put the pan on a wire rack and let cool about 10 minutes before serving.

Tightly covered and stored on the refrigerator, Tempeh "Croutons" will keep for 3 days.

TASTY TOFU BITES

Makes 4 servings ■ **Prep Time:** 10 minutes / **Bake Time:** 25 to 30 minutes /
Refrigeration Time: 3 to 4 hours (optional)

These petite little tofu cubes can be featured in numerous dishes. Top a simple green salad with these tasty tidbits to add protein and substance *or* use them to enhance stir-fries, casseroles, or even soups.

1 block (15 to 16 ounces) super-firm *or* extra-firm regular tofu (refrigerated package or tub), drained and cut into ½-inch cubes (pressing first is not required)

1 tablespoon gluten-free tamari *or* coconut aminos

1 tablespoon maple syrup

1 tablespoon extra-virgin olive oil

½ rounded teaspoon smoked paprika

Preheat the oven to 425°F. Line a small, rimmed baking sheet with unbleached parchment paper.

Put the tofu cubes into a medium-sized bowl. Put the tamari, maple syrup, olive oil, and paprika into a small bowl and briskly whisk to combine. Pour the sauce over the tofu and gently toss, using a large spoon, until the tofu cubes are coated with the sauce.

Arrange the tofu cubes in a single layer on the lined baking sheet. Bake for 25 to 30 minutes, turning once, until the edges of the tofu have become crispy and golden brown. Cool for 5 minutes and serve, or cover and refrigerate for 3 to 4 hours and serve cold.

Laura serves *Chickpea & Artichoke Salad* (page 48)

*Pumpkin Pie Spiced
Butternut Squash Soup*
(page 76)

HEARTY SOUPS & STEWS

Nourishing, hearty soups are a staple for many of us during the colder months, but soup can certainly be served the whole year through. From lentil, squash, and veggie soups, to a hearty chili and summer berry soup, this festive potage variety will make soup meals into fun meals!

LENTIL & CAULIFLOWER CURRY SOUP

Makes 6 to 8 servings ■ **Prep Time:** 20 minutes / **Stove Top:** 48 to 52 minutes

Yummy red lentils combined with flavorful fire-roasted tomatoes cook down to make this cauliflower curry soup flavorful, thick and creamy. Hearty and delicious, this soup makes a welcome entrée any night of the week!

1¼ cups red lentils, sorted and rinsed

1 can (14 to 15 ounces) diced fire-roasted tomatoes, with juice

7 cups cauliflower florets (about 1 medium head)

1 medium sweet onion, sliced or chopped

4 cups cubed white or yellow potatoes (peeling is optional)

1 tablespoon mild curry powder

½ teaspoon salt

8 cups very strong vegetable broth (see Chef's Note)

1 cup water

1 tablespoon extra-virgin olive oil

8 cups (loosely packed) baby spinach

Put the lentils, tomatoes, cauliflower, onion, potatoes, curry powder, salt, vegetable broth, and water in a large soup pot over medium-high heat. Cover loosely and bring to a boil.

Decrease the heat to medium-low, cover, and simmer, stirring occasionally, for 40 minutes. Add the olive oil and spinach and cook, stirring occasionally, for 8 to 12 minutes more. Serve hot.

CHEF'S NOTE

■ You may use 9 cups water and 2 large crumbled vegan gluten-free bouillon cubes in place of the 8 cups vegetable broth and the 1 cup water, if desired.

RED LENTIL & BABY BOK CHOY SOUP

Makes 6 servings ▪ **Prep Time:** 20 minutes / **Stove Top:** 60 to 75 minutes

A humble combination of red lentils and baby bok choy produces a robust soup with delicate flavors that you can adjust to suit your family's tastes.

1¼ cups red lentils, sorted and rinsed

1 large can (28 ounces) diced fire-roasted tomatoes, with juice

2½ to 3 cups sliced baby bok choy stalks (from about 2 large heads or 3 to 5 small heads, see Chef's Note)

¾ cup chopped red or sweet onion

1 heaping tablespoon mild curry powder (see Variations)

1 tablespoon extra-virgin olive oil

1 tablespoon gluten-free tamari *or* coconut aminos

½ teaspoon garlic powder

6 cups water

2 cups (firmly packed) thinly sliced baby bok choy leaves (see Chef's Note)

Salt, to taste

Put the lentils, tomatoes, baby bok choy *stalks*, onion, curry powder, olive oil, tamari, garlic powder, and water in a large soup pot. Cover and bring to a simmer over medium-high heat.

Decrease the heat to medium-low, cover, and simmer, stirring occasionally, for 50 minutes to 1 hour. Add the sliced baby bok choy *leaves* and cook, stirring occasionally, for 10 to 15 minutes more. Taste and add salt, if desired. Serve hot with *Vegan Buttermilk Cornbread* (page 38) or *Piña Colada Muffins* (page 34) on the side, if desired.

VARIATIONS

▪ **Italian Red Lentil Soup:** To give the soup an Italian flair, you may replace all of the curry powder with 1 heaping tablespoon *Italian Seasoning Blend* (page 112). Proceed with recipe as directed.

▪ **Red Lentil, Potato, and Baby Bok Choy Soup:** For a heartier and thicker soup, add 2 cups cubed red or white potatoes (leave peels on) when you add the lentils to the soup. Proceed with recipe as directed.

■ To prepare baby bok choy, start by cutting off the tough root end from each head of baby bok choy. Remove any discolored leaves, separate the stalks, and place in a bowl of water. Swish the stalks to loosen bits of dirt from the stalks. Put the stalks in a large colander, rinse well under cold running water and then drain. Gather the clean stalks into a bunch, put them on a cutting board and slice the stalks crosswise, starting at the root end. When you get to the tender green leaves, roll them up and cut across into thin slices. At this point, thoroughly rinse the bok choy stalk slices *and* leaves again (in separate colanders) under cold running water, to be certain all of the sand and dirt is *thoroughly* removed.

GARAM MASALA SPICED SPLIT PEA SOUP

Makes 6 servings ■ **Prep Time:** 20 minutes / **Stove Top:** 1½ to 2 hours

Hearty split peas and garam masala combined with celery, carrots, and sweet potatoes creates a satisfying potage for a nourishing family meal.

1 pound dried split peas, sorted and rinsed

2 cups sliced carrots (peeling is optional)

2 cups sliced celery, with leaves

1½ cups peeled and chopped sweet potatoes

1 large sweet onion, chopped

1 tablespoon gluten-free tamari *or* coconut aminos

1½ teaspoons garam masala

¼ teaspoon salt, plus more as needed

⅛ teaspoon cayenne pepper

10 cups water, plus more as needed

Put all of the ingredients in a large soup pot. Cover, and bring to a simmer over medium-high heat. Decrease the heat to medium-low and simmer for 1½ to 2 hours, stirring occasionally, until the soup is thick and the split peas and vegetables are soft. Add more water, as needed, if the soup becomes too thick as it cooks. Taste and add more salt, if desired. Serve hot, with *Coco-nutty Apple Muffins* (page 32) and/or *Simple Supper Salad* (page 59) on the side, if desired.

Put any leftover soup in a tightly covered container and refrigerate up to 3 days. The soup will thicken considerably as it chills. Before reheating, stir the soup thoroughly and add more water (or vegetable broth) as needed, to thin the soup out to the desired consistency.

TASTY CHICKEN-LESS SOUP

Makes 6 to 8 servings ■ **Prep Time:** 25 minutes / **Stove Top:** 50 to 55 minutes

This delicious soup incorporates many of the flavors in classic chicken soup, without the chicken!

10 to 12 baby white and/
or red potatoes, sliced
or chopped (peeling is
optional)

6 medium carrots, sliced
(peeling is optional)

½ medium bunch celery,
with leaves, sliced

8 ounces white
button or cremini
mushrooms, sliced

1 large sweet onion, sliced

1½ large vegan
gluten-free bouillon
cubes, crumbled

1 tablespoon extra-virgin
olive oil

½ tablespoon gluten-free
tamari *or* coconut
aminos, plus more
as needed

Water, as needed

Salt, to taste (optional)

*Flavorful Brown Basmati
Rice*, optional, (page 190)

Put the potatoes, carrots, celery, mushrooms, onion, bouillon cubes, olive oil, and tamari in a large soup pot. Add water to cover the vegetables by 1 to 2 inches. Cover and bring to a simmer over medium-high heat.

Decrease the heat to medium-low, cover, and simmer, stirring occasionally, for 50 to 55 minutes (see note for Variation). Taste and add more tamari or season with salt, if desired. Serve hot, in deep soup bowls, spooned over a generous serving of (optional) *Flavorful Brown Basmati Rice.*

VARIATION

■ **Tasty Tofu Chicken-less Soup:** If a heartier soup is desired, add 1 to 1½ cups cubed, extra-firm regular or super-firm tofu during the last 20 minutes of cooking the soup.

PUMPKIN PIE SPICED BUTTERNUT SQUASH SOUP

Makes 4 to 6 servings ■ **Prep Time:** 70 minutes / **Stove Top:** 15 minutes

I like to serve this easy and impressive soup during the winter holidays, but it is wonderful to serve any time of year. An extra pop of cinnamon and some sweet maple syrup both add zing to this smooth and flavorful potage.

5½ cups cubed butternut squash, (about 1 medium squash, peeled, seeded and cut into 1- to 1½-inch pieces)

1 tablespoon extra-virgin olive oil

2 tablespoons maple syrup, divided

Scant ¼ teaspoon pumpkin pie spice (see Chef's Note)

2 cups sweetened *or* unsweetened plain dairy-free milk, plus more as needed

¼ teaspoon salt, plus more as needed

⅛ rounded teaspoon ground cinnamon, plus more for garnish

Pinch (about ⅟₁₆ teaspoon) cayenne pepper (optional)

Preheat the oven to 400°F. Line a large, rimmed baking sheet with unbleached parchment paper.

Put the cubed squash, olive oil, 1 tablespoon maple syrup, and pumpkin pie spice in a large bowl and toss gently until thoroughly coated. Arrange the squash in a single layer on the prepared pan. Bake for 40 to 45 minutes, stirring once or twice, until the squash is soft and slightly golden. Put the pan on a wire rack. Let the squash cool for 15 to 20 minutes (see Chef's Note).

Put the cooled roasted squash, dairy-free milk, 1 tablespoon maple syrup, ¼ teaspoon salt, cinnamon, and optional pinch of cayenne pepper in a blender and process until smooth and creamy, adding more dairy-free milk or water, 3 to 4 tablespoons at a time, as needed, to achieve the desired consistency (see Chef's Note).

Pour the soup into a medium-sized saucepan, cover and cook over medium-low heat for about 15 minutes, stirring often, until heated through. To serve, ladle the soup into small bowls and sprinkle each bowl with a pinch of cinnamon. Serve hot.

- If desired, use *Mom's Pumpkin Pie Spice* (page 110) *or* replace all of the pumpkin pie spice with ground cinnamon.

- You may roast the squash up to 24 hours ahead of time. After cooling, transfer to an airtight container and refrigerate until use.

- This soup may be made up to 24 hours ahead of time. If making in advance, let the soup cool after blending, then pour the cooled soup into an airtight container and refrigerate. To reheat the soup, pour it into a pot. The soup will thicken considerably when chilled, so before re-heating, add a bit more dairy-free milk or water to achieve the desired consistency. Cook for about 15 to 20 minutes over medium-low heat, stirring very often, until heated through.

ZUCCHINI-TOMATO SOUP
WITH ROOT VEGGIES

Makes 6 servings ▪ **Prep Time:** 20 minutes / **Stove Top:** 45 to 55 minutes

A few root veggies combined with tender zucchini and lentils makes a robust, tomato-based soup for a hearty family meal.

1 cup red lentils, sorted and rinsed

1 large can (28 ounces) diced fire-roasted tomatoes, with juice

3 medium russet or yellow potatoes, peeled and cubed

3 medium-large carrots, sliced or chopped (peeling is optional)

1 medium-large zucchini, cut into cubes (do not peel)

1 medium red or yellow onion, chopped

1½ tablespoons mild curry powder (see Variation)

1 tablespoon extra-virgin olive oil

1 large vegan gluten-free bouillon cube, crumbled

¼ rounded teaspoon salt, plus more if needed

8 to 9 cups water, plus more as needed

Put the lentils, tomatoes with juice, potatoes, carrots, zucchini, onion, curry powder, olive oil, bouillon cube, and salt in a large soup pot. Add 8 to 9 cups water to cover veggies by 1 to 2 inches. Cover and bring to a simmer over medium-high heat.

Decrease the heat to medium-low, cover, and simmer, stirring occasionally, for 45 to 55 minutes or until the veggies and lentils are soft. Taste and add more salt, if desired. Serve with your favorite crackers and crisp green salad on the side, if desired.

VARIATION

▪ **Italian-Style Zucchini-Tomato Soup:** To give the soup an Italian flair, you may replace all of the curry powder with 1 to 1½ tablespoons *Italian Seasoning Blend* (page 112). Proceed with recipe as directed.

BUTTERNUT-VEGGIE SOUP

Makes 6 to 8 servings ▪ **Prep Time:** 30 minutes / **Stove Top:** 50 minutes to 1 hour

Butternut squash combined with garden-fresh veggies makes a low-fat but filling combination that's simple to prepare for a hearty weeknight meal.

½ large butternut squash, peeled, seeded, and cut into 1- to 1½ -inch cubes

6 to 7 large carrots, sliced (peeling is optional)

½ medium bunch celery, with leaves, sliced

8 ounces white button or cremini mushrooms, sliced

1 medium sweet onion, sliced

1½ large vegan gluten-free bouillon cubes, crumbled

Water, as needed

Salt, to taste

Put all of the squash, carrots, celery, mushrooms, onion, and bouillon cubes in a large soup pot. Add water to cover the vegetables by 1 to 2 inches. Cover and bring to a simmer over medium-high heat.

Decrease the heat to medium-low, cover, and simmer, stirring occasionally, for 50 minutes to 1 hour. Taste and add salt, if desired. Serve hot, in deep soup bowls with green salad on the side, if desired.

"MEATY" TWO-BEAN VEGAN CHILI

Makes 4 servings ■ **Prep Time:** 20 minutes / **Stove Top:** 96 to 108 minutes

This slightly spicy and totally satisfying chili uses vegan burger patties in place of meat to add authentic flavor along with a hearty texture. This is my hubby's favorite jazzy chili!

1 medium yellow or sweet onion, sliced

2 tablespoons extra-virgin olive oil, divided

2 tablespoons gluten-free tamari *or* coconut aminos, divided

1 tablespoon plus 1 teaspoon chili powder, divided

1 teaspoon garlic powder

7 tablespoons water, plus more as needed, divided

4 frozen, gluten-free, vegan burgers or 12 to 14 ounces gluten-free, vegan beefless ground crumbles (see Chef's Note and see Variation)

1 can (28 ounces) diced tomatoes, with juice

1 can (15 to 16 ounces) white beans, drained and rinsed (your preferred variety)

1 can (15 to 16 ounces) red kidney beans, drained and rinsed

¼ rounded teaspoon freshly ground black pepper

Put the onion, 1 tablespoon olive oil, 1 tablespoon tamari, ½ tablespoon chili powder, and 1 teaspoon garlic powder into a soup pot and cook over medium-high heat for 3 minutes, stirring often. Add 3 tablespoons of water, cover and cook for 3 to 5 minutes, stirring occasionally, adding a *bit* more water if the pan becomes dry.

Add the frozen burgers, 4 tablespoons water, and 1 tablespoon olive oil. Cover and cook for about 10 minutes, breaking up the burgers into chunks with the back of a large spoon, and adding a *bit* more water if the pan becomes dry.

Add the diced tomatoes with juice, white beans, kidney beans, 1 tablespoon tamari, ½ tablespoon plus 1 teaspoon chili powder, and ¼ rounded teaspoon

continued on the next page ➤

freshly ground black pepper and stir to combine. Cover, and bring the chili to a slow simmer.

Decrease the heat to medium-low, cover loosely, and cook for 80 to 90 minutes, stirring occasionally, or until the chili is thickening up. Serve the chili in wide soup bowls topped with *Laura's Vegan Sour Cream* (page 107) and *Vegan Buttermilk Cornbread* (page 38) on the side, if desired.

CHEF'S NOTE

■ I like the "chipotle-style" burgers for this recipe.

VARIATION

■ **Two-Bean Butternut Squash Chili:** Replace the vegan burgers with 3½ to 4 cups peeled, seeded, and cubed butternut squash cut into 1- to 1½-inch cubes. Leave the squash cubes whole in the chili. (Do not mash them up.) Proceed with recipe as directed.

Laura serves *"Meaty" Two-Bean Vegan Chili*

EASY VEGETABLE & TOFU SOUP

Makes 4 to 6 servings ■ **Prep Time:** 20 minutes / **Stove Top:** 50 to 55 minutes

This soup is brimming with root vegetables and celery, with tofu added for texture and extra protein. Hearty and nutritious to serve as a main course for supper, it makes a satisfying luncheon entrée, too.

1 small bunch celery, with leaves, chopped

5 large carrots, chopped (peeling is optional)

4 large red potatoes, peeled and chopped

1½ teaspoons Italian seasoning blend

6 cups vegetable broth

2 cups water, plus more as needed

1 block (14 to 16 ounces) extra-firm regular tofu (refrigerated tub), drained and cubed

2 teaspoons gluten-free tamari *or* coconut aminos

2 cups (firmly packed) baby spinach, rough chopped

Salt, to taste

Freshly ground black pepper, to taste

Put the celery, carrots, potatoes, and Italian seasoning in a large soup pot. Add the broth and 2 cups water. Add more water, if needed, to cover the vegetables by 1 to 2 inches. Cover and bring to a simmer over medium-high heat.

Decrease the heat to medium-low, cover, and simmer, stirring occasionally, for 35 to 40 minutes.

While the soup cooks, put the tofu into a medium-sized bowl and drizzle with the tamari. Toss to coat. Cover and refrigerate for 20 to 25 minutes.

Add the tofu with the tamari to the pot and simmer, stirring occasionally, for 10 minutes. Add the baby spinach and simmer for 5 minutes more. Season with salt and pepper to taste. Serve hot.

FRESH BLUEBERRY-VANILLA SOUP
WITH VEGAN ORANGE CREAM

Makes 4 to 5 servings ■ **Prep Time:** 20 minutes / **Refrigeration Time:** 3 to 4 hours

Fresh puréed blueberries enhanced with a generous swirl of flavorful vegan orange cashew "cream" makes a cool summer soup to serve for a lovely first course or refreshing dessert!

VEGAN ORANGE CREAM

⅔ cup plus 2 tablespoons raw cashews (soaked, drained, and rinsed, see Chef's Note)

1 cup freshly squeezed orange juice, plus more if needed (zest the oranges first)

1½ tablespoons maple syrup

Water, if needed

BLUEBERRY-VANILLA SOUP

3½ cups fresh blueberries

1 cup unsweetened *or* sweetened vanilla flavored dairy-free milk, plus more as needed

2 tablespoons maple syrup

Orange zest, for garnish (optional)

VEGAN ORANGE CREAM

To make the cream, put the soaked and drained cashews, orange juice, and 1½ tablespoons maple syrup into a blender and process until very smooth, adding more orange juice or some water, if needed, to achieve desired consistency. Transfer the cream to a covered container and refrigerate for 3 to 4 hours, until completely cold.

BLUEBERRY-VANILLA SOUP

To make the soup, put the blueberries, dairy-free milk, and 2 tablespoons maple syrup into a blender and process until *very* smooth. Transfer to a covered container and refrigerate for 3 to 4 hours, until completely cold. The soup will thicken and separate while it chills. Right before serving, put the blueberry soup back into the blender and process until it becomes a smooth purée again, adding a bit more vanilla-flavored dairy-free milk, if needed, to achieve desired consistency.

To serve, divide the blueberry soup into 4 to 6 small bowls. Swirl a very generous amount of the vegan orange cream into the top of each soup and garnish with optional orange zest. Put the

continued on page 87 ➤

remaining vegan orange cream in a small pitcher to pass around the table so that diners can add more "cream" to their soup, if desired (see Chef's Note).

CHEF'S NOTES

■ To soak the cashews, put the raw cashews and ½ cup water into a small bowl. Refrigerate for 1 to 4 hours. Drain the cashews and rinse thoroughly in cold water. Proceed as directed.

■ Tightly covered and refrigerated, leftover *Vegan Orange Cream* will keep for 2 to 3 days. It will thicken up considerably in the refrigerator. To thin to desired consistency, add a bit more orange juice or water, and stir to combine. Bonus: *Vegan Orange Cream* is delicious served drizzled over cake or pie, too!

Four-Veggie Salad
(page 92)

LET'S GET SAUCY!

Nothin' like a little sauce to jazz up a meal! Dressings, dipping sauces, pasta sauces, creamy sauces, and snazzy seasonings bring family meals alive with plant-based flavor.

SWEET & SPICY DRESSING

Makes about ⅔ cup dressing ■ **Prep Time:** 5 minutes

A little bit of sweet mixed with a little bit of spice dresses up a veggie salad, chickpea salad, pasta salad, or *Artichoke, Olive, and Potato Salad* (page 47).

⅓ cup vegan mayonnaise or *Quick Vegan Mayonnaise* (page 108)

4 tablespoons spicy brown or Dijon mustard

2 tablespoons maple syrup

1 teaspoon smoked paprika

¼ teaspoon ground turmeric

¼ teaspoon salt

⅛ teaspoon cayenne pepper

Put all of the ingredients into a small bowl and briskly whisk to combine.

ITALIAN-STYLE LEMON DRESSING

Makes about ½ cup dressing ■ **Prep Time:** 5 minutes

My go-to when flavoring many dishes is often Italian seasoning. This Italian inspired dressing is quick to assemble and pairs well with a crisp green salad or grain salad.

4 tablespoons freshly squeezed lemon juice

2 tablespoons extra-virgin olive oil

1 tablespoon maple syrup

1 teaspoon Italian seasoning blend

¼ teaspoon salt

Freshly ground black pepper, to taste (optional)

Pinch (about ¹⁄₁₆ teaspoon) cayenne pepper

Put all of the ingredients into a small bowl and briskly whisk to emulsify.

BALSAMIC-ORANGE DRESSING

Makes about ⅔ cup dressing ■ **Prep Time:** 5 minutes

This dressing is a tasty variation on my "go-to" dressing. It's the perfect blend of tangy and sweet, making it an ideal choice for any crisp green salad.

4 tablespoons orange (or tangerine) infused extra-virgin olive oil (see Variations)

3 tablespoons maple syrup

2 tablespoons Dijon mustard

2 tablespoons good-quality balsamic vinegar

Put all of the ingredients into a small bowl and briskly whisk to emulsify.

VARIATIONS

■ **Sweet Balsamic-Dijon Salad Dressing:** Replace the orange infused extra-virgin olive oil with plain extra-virgin olive oil. This is my "go-to" dressing!

■ **Balsamic-Lemon Dressing:** Replace the orange infused extra-virgin olive oil with lemon infused extra-virgin olive oil.

SERVING SUGGESTION

■ **Four-Veggie Salad:** For a quick family-style salad, artfully arrange chopped Romaine lettuce, grape tomatoes, carrot sticks, and sweet pepper slices in a salad bowl. Drizzle with *Balsamic-Orange Dressing* and several generous grinds of rainbow black pepper (optional), and serve (shown on page 88).

MAPLE-LIME DRESSING

Makes about ½ cup dressing ■ **Prep Time:** 5 minutes

A generous pop of maple syrup combined with tart lime results in a refreshing dressing that will bring any green salad alive with flavor! Enhanced with a touch of garlic powder and smoked paprika, this recipe can perk up hearty main-dish salads, too—like my *Minty Quinoa Salad* (page 51).

3½ tablespoons freshly squeezed lime juice

2 tablespoons extra-virgin olive oil

2 tablespoons maple syrup

1 tablespoon good-quality balsamic vinegar

½ teaspoon salt

¼ teaspoon garlic powder

¼ teaspoon smoked paprika

Freshly ground black pepper, to taste (optional)

Put all of the ingredients into a small bowl and briskly whisk to emulsify.

LEMON-SHALLOT DRESSING

Makes about ½ cup dressing ■ **Prep Time:** 5 minutes

Shallots provide zing, lemon juice adds tang, and maple syrup imparts a touch of sweet to this inviting dressing. Dress up a baby spring greens salad or *Quinoa and Curly Parsley Bowl* (page 52) with this flavorful vinaigrette.

4½ tablespoons freshly squeezed lemon juice

3 tablespoons extra-virgin olive oil

1 tablespoon maple syrup

1 tablespoon good-quality balsamic vinegar

½ teaspoon garlic powder

¼ teaspoon salt

1/16 teaspoon cayenne pepper

1 rounded tablespoon finely minced shallots

Put all of the ingredients except the shallots into a small bowl and briskly whisk to emulsify. Add the shallots and stir to combine.

SWEET & TANGY TAHINI DRESSING

Makes about 1 cup dressing ■ **Prep Time:** 5 minutes

This tangy twist on a favorite vegan dressing will dress up any green salad, steamed veggie combo, cooked grains, or a main dish entrée like *Laura's Buddha Bowl* (page 161, shown served on the opposite page).

¼ cup freshly squeezed lemon juice

2 tablespoons maple syrup

6 rounded tablespoons sesame tahini

2 to 3 tablespoons water, plus more as needed

Put the lemon juice and maple syrup into a small bowl and briskly whisk to combine. Add the tahini and 2 tablespoons water, and whisk vigorously until creamy, adding more water to achieve desired consistency. (Use less water for a thicker consistency, more water for a thinner consistency.)

SMOKY & SPICY BURGER SAUCE

Makes about ⅓ cup ▪ **Prep Time:** 5 minutes

Simple, smoky, spicy, *and* sweet, this sauce dresses up vegan burgers like *Rockin' Black Bean Burgers* (page 158, shown served on the opposite page), but is equally wonderful served with sandwiches, steamed veggies, or green salads, too!

4 heaping tablespoons vegan mayonnaise or *Quick Vegan Mayonnaise* (page 108)

2 heaping tablespoons prepared ketchup, plus more to taste

¼ teaspoon smoked paprika

¼ teaspoon sriracha-style hot sauce (use ½ teaspoon or more for extra spicy)

Put all of the ingredients into a small bowl and whisk to combine. Add more ketchup, if desired and stir to combine.

MAPLE-MUSTARD DIPPING SAUCE

Makes ½ cup plus 1 tablespoon ■ **Prep Time:** 5 minutes

This dandy dipping sauce is my vegan version of the snazzy sauce served at fast food eateries. Offer this zippy dip with *Oven-Fried Tofu Nuggets* (page 121, shown served on the opposite page) or *Pecan-Crusted Zucchini Filets* (page 141).

¼ cup vegan mayonnaise or *Quick Vegan Mayonnaise* (page 108)

3 tablespoons Dijon mustard

2 tablespoons maple syrup

Put all of the ingredients into a small bowl and stir to combine. Cover and refrigerate until serving.

CLASSIC COCKTAIL SAUCE

Makes about ⅓ cup ▪ **Prep Time:** 5 minutes

This zingy sauce makes a fantastic dip to jazz up vegan crab cakes, *Oven-Fried Tofu Nuggets* (page 121) or *Polenta Cottage Fries* (page 193).

───────────────────────────────

¼ cup ketchup

1½ tablespoons prepared horseradish, plus more as needed

1 teaspoon freshly squeezed lemon juice

Put all of the sauce ingredients into a small bowl. Stir to combine. Taste and add more horseradish, if desired. Cover and refrigerate until serving.

EASY MARINARA SAUCE

Makes 4 servings ■ **Prep Time:** 5 minutes / **Stove Top:** 30 to 45 minutes

Use this simple sauce to flavor an Italian-style casserole or spoon it over pasta or zoodles for a satisfying supper dish.

1 can (26 to 28 ounces) regular or fire-roasted crushed tomatoes

1 tablespoon extra-virgin olive oil

1 tablespoon gluten-free tamari *or* coconut aminos

2 teaspoons Italian seasoning blend

½ teaspoon garlic powder

½ teaspoon crushed red pepper flakes

¼ teaspoon salt

Put all of the ingredients into a medium-sized saucepan and stir with a large spoon until combined (see Chef's Note). Cover and bring to a simmer over medium-high heat. Decrease the heat to medium-low and simmer for 30 to 45 minutes.

CHEF'S NOTE

■ If you are using this sauce in a casserole (or lasagna), there is no need to cook it first! Simply put all of the ingredients in a bowl and stir together to combine. Add the sauce to your recipe when you are assembling it for the oven. SO *easy*!

CHUNKY MUSHROOM MARINARA SAUCE

Makes 4 to 6 servings ▪ **Prep Time:** 20 minutes / **Stove Top:** 50 to 60 minutes

When a hearty marinara sauce is required, this tasty sauce fills the bill. Adding the tamari and spices a little at a time develops layers of flavor in this oh-so-appetizing sauce.

2 small yellow onions, chopped

1 tablespoon extra-virgin olive oil

2 tablespoons plus 1 teaspoon gluten-free tamari *or* coconut aminos, divided

8 ounces cremini mushrooms, sliced

3 teaspoons Italian seasoning blend, divided

2½ tablespoons water, plus more as needed, divided

2 small red or orange sweet bell peppers, seeded and chopped

1 can (26 to 28 ounces) crushed tomatoes

½ teaspoon garlic powder

Scant ⅛ teaspoon crushed red pepper

Put the onions, 1 tablespoon olive oil, and 1 tablespoon tamari into a large sauté pan. Cover and cook over medium heat for 10 minutes stirring occasionally. Add the mushrooms, 1 teaspoon Italian seasoning, 1 teaspoon tamari, and 1½ tablespoons water. Cover and cook for 7 minutes, stirring occasionally, adding 1 tablespoon of water if the pan becomes dry.

Add the bell peppers and cook for 5 to 7 minutes, stirring occasionally. Add the tomatoes, 1 tablespoon tamari, 2 teaspoons Italian seasoning, garlic powder, and crushed red pepper. Pour 1 tablespoon water into the tomato can and slosh it around to loosen the remaining crushed tomatoes and add the "tomato water" to the pan.

Decrease the heat to medium-low. Cover and cook, stirring occasionally, for 35 to 45 minutes or until the sauce has cooked down and is thickened. Serve over your favorite rice or pasta, or use it on *Spaghetti Squash Bowls* (page 171, shown served on the opposite page).

LAURA'S VEGAN SOUR CREAM

Makes about ¾ cup ■ **Prep Time:** 5 minutes

This authentic tasting, easy, and delicious vegan sour "cream" can be used in place of the dairy variety in any recipe that calls for sour cream. Add a generous dollop to *"Meaty" Two-Bean Vegan Chili* (page 81, shown served on the opposite page).

½ cup raw cashews, (soaked, drained, and rinsed, see Chef's Note)

¼ cup water, plus more as needed

1½ tablespoons freshly squeezed lemon juice

⅛ teaspoon salt, plus more if needed

Put the soaked and drained cashews, ¼ cup water, lemon juice, and salt into a blender and process until smooth and creamy. If a thinner sour cream is desired, add up to 2 additional tablespoons water. Taste and add more salt if desired. Stored tightly covered in the refrigerator, the vegan sour cream will keep for up to 2 days.

CHEF'S NOTE

■ To soak the cashews, put the cashews and ⅓ cup water into a small bowl. Refrigerate for 1 to 4 hours. Drain the cashews and rinse thoroughly in cold water.

QUICK VEGAN MAYONNAISE

Makes about 1¼ cups ■ **Prep Time:** 10 minutes

There are several tasty brands of store bought mayonnaise, but if you are seeking a delicious homemade version, this speedy recipe certainly fills the bill.

¾ cup raw cashews
(see Chef's Note)

½ cup water, plus more
as needed

1 tablespoon freshly
squeezed lemon juice

2 teaspoons Dijon or spicy
brown mustard

1¼ teaspoons vegan cane
sugar or your preferred
dry sweetener

Put all of the ingredients in a blender and process until smooth, adding more water, 2 tablespoons at a time to achieve the desired consistency. Refrigerate for 2 to 4 hours until chilled.

CHEF'S NOTE

■ If desired, you *may* soak the cashews first. Put the cashews and ½ cup water into a small bowl. Refrigerate for 1 to 4 hours. Drain the cashews and rinse thoroughly in cold water. Proceed with recipe as directed.

VEGAN CHIVE RICOTTA

Makes 4 to 5 servings ▪ **Prep Time:** 10 minutes

This flavorful and quick-to-prepare "ricotta" works beautifully layered in casseroles or sprinkled over salads, and it's a real standout in *Eggplant Lasagna with Vegan Chive Ricotta* (page 129) or any lasagna dish you may be serving your family.

1 block (15 to 16 ounces) extra-firm regular tofu (refrigerated tub), well-drained and broken into chunks

⅓ cup (firmly packed) chopped fresh chives

1 tablespoon extra-virgin olive oil

2 teaspoons gluten-free tamari *or* coconut aminos

½ teaspoon garlic powder

⅛ teaspoon salt (see Chef's Note)

Several grinds of black pepper

Put the tofu, chives, olive oil, tamari, garlic powder, salt, and a few grinds of freshly ground pepper into a medium-sized bowl. Mash to the consistency of chunky ricotta cheese using a potato masher or large fork. Covered and refrigerated, *Vegan Chive Ricotta* will keep for 1 day.

CHEF'S NOTE
▪ For a saltier vegan ricotta, add an additional ⅛ teaspoon salt.

VARIATION
▪ **Vegan Basil Ricotta**: Substitute ⅓ cup chopped fresh basil for the chives.

MOM'S PUMPKIN PIE SPICE

Makes ¼ cup ■ **Prep Time:** 5 minutes

This spice combination is one of my mom's wonderful recipes. It showcases the perfect blend of flavors to enhance any pumpkin pie, cookie, cake, or soup that calls for a classic sweet-and-spicy taste. Try it in *Pumpkin Pie Breakfast Rice* (page 22), *Date-Nut Snowballs* (page 259, shown on the opposite page), *Pumpkin-Pecan Pie* (page 254), or *Pumpkin Pie Spiced Butternut Squash Soup* (page 76).

1 tablespoon ground cinnamon

1 tablespoon ground ginger

1 tablespoon ground nutmeg

1 tablespoon ground allspice

Put all of the ingredients into a small bowl and stir with a dry whisk to combine. Store in a tightly sealed container in a dry place away from sunlight.

LAURA'S ITALIAN SEASONING BLEND

Makes about 5 tablespoons ▪ **Prep Time:** 5 minutes

Here's my delicious version of traditional Italian-style seasoning. Add your family's favorite dried herbs to create your own tasty blend. You can use this flavorsome seasoning anytime a recipe in this book calls for *Italian Seasoning Blend* such as *Big Protein Quinoa Casserole* (page 116, shown served on the opposite page).

2 tablespoons dried basil

5 teaspoons dried oregano

3 teaspoons dried marjoram

1 teaspoon dried thyme

1 teaspoon dried crushed rosemary

½ teaspoon dried rubbed sage

Put all of the ingredients into a small bowl and stir to thoroughly combine. Store in a tightly sealed container in a dry place away from sunlight.

BBQ Tempeh Triangles
(page 136)

*Roasted Zucchini Slices
and Smoky Summer
Squash Slices*
(page 198)

Red Potato Oven Fries
(page 176)

CASSEROLES & SHEET PAN SUPPERS

Chop it up, mix it up, and put it in the oven. What could be simpler? The key to easy meals is to start with easy prep and end with quick clean-up. The delicious main dishes in this chapter are baked in a casserole dish in the oven or arranged on a sheet pan and roasted to perfection. All of these hearty entrées are designed to please the entire family.

BIG PROTEIN QUINOA CASSEROLE

Makes 4 servings ■ **Prep Time:** 30 minutes / **Bake Time:** 55 to 65 minutes

Protein-rich tempeh takes the lead, enhanced with quinoa and cashews to provide a delicious casserole that's substantial *and* nutritious, sure to become a family-favorite at your supper table.

1 block (8 ounces) tempeh, cut into 1-inch cubes

2 cups vegetable broth, divided, plus more as needed

2 tablespoons extra-virgin olive oil, divided

3½ teaspoons Italian seasoning blend, divided

2 cups shredded or grated carrots

2 cups cooked quinoa or *Laura's Easy Quinoa* (page 194) (see Chef's Note)

¾ cup diced sweet onion

½ cup chopped, roasted, and salted cashews

¼ cup frozen green peas

¼ teaspoon salt

Preheat the oven to 400°F.

Put the tempeh and ½ cup vegetable broth into a sauté pan. Cover and bring to a simmer over medium-high heat. Decrease the heat to medium and let the tempeh "steam" for 7 to 8 minutes. Add another ½ cup vegetable broth, 1 tablespoon oil, and ½ teaspoon Italian seasoning blend. Cover and cook, stirring occasionally, for 10 minutes.

Meanwhile, put the carrots, quinoa, onion, cashews, peas, 3 teaspoons Italian seasoning blend, and salt into a large bowl and gently stir, using a large spoon, until combined. Add the cooked tempeh and gently stir to combine.

Transfer the mixture to a 10- to 12-cup (or similarly sized) casserole dish. Pour 1 cup vegetable broth over the mixture. Cover and bake for 30 minutes.

Carefully uncover the casserole (steam will be *very, very hot!*) and drizzle with 1 tablespoon oil (optional) over the top. Add ¼ cup broth if the mixture seems dry at this point. Cover and bake for 25 to 35 more, or until the veggies are cooked and casserole is bubbling hot, checking often and adding 2 tablespoons more of the broth if bottom of casserole seems dry. Uncover and let stand for 5 to 10 minutes before serving. Serve warm.

BAKED TOFU ITALIANO

Makes 4 servings ■ **Prep Time:** 20 minutes / **Bake Time:** 40 to 45 minutes

With a true Italian flair, this easy casserole is a great way to introduce tofu to folks who are skeptical about tofu. This dish prepares for the oven in under 20 minutes, making it an ideal weeknight supper option.

2 tablespoons extra-virgin olive oil, divided

1 large sweet onion, thinly sliced

2 tablespoons gluten-free tamari *or* coconut aminos, divided

½ teaspoon garlic powder, divided

1 block (16 ounces) super-firm regular tofu (refrigerated package or tub, see Chef's Note), drained

1 can (15 to 16 ounces) fire roasted, plain, or basil-flavored diced tomatoes, with juice

1 teaspoon Italian seasoning blend

⅛ teaspoon crushed red pepper

Preheat the oven to 400°F. Spread 1 tablespoon olive oil evenly over the bottom of a 9- x 12-inch (or similarly sized) casserole dish.

Put the onion, 1 tablespoon olive oil, 1 tablespoon tamari, and ¼ teaspoon garlic powder in a large sauté pan. Cover and cook over medium heat, stirring often, for 10 minutes, or until the edges of the onion slices are golden.

Cut the tofu into 10 "cutlets" by first slicing it down the middle, then turning each half on its side and then slicing each half into five thin "cutlets." Arrange the tofu "cutlets" in an even layer over the olive oil in the casserole dish. Top the tofu with all of the sautéed onions. Pour the diced tomatoes with juice evenly over the tofu and onion mixture. Drizzle 1 tablespoon of tamari evenly over the diced tomatoes. Sprinkle the Italian seasoning blend, ¼ teaspoon garlic powder and crushed red pepper over the tomatoes.

Cover tightly and bake for 40 to 45 minutes or until the casserole is bubbling and the tofu begins to get golden around the edges. Put the dish on a wire rack and let cool about 10 minutes before serving with *Lemony Broccoli with Sunflower Seeds* (page 208) and *Quick Quinoa with Mushrooms* (page 189) on the side (shown on the opposite page), if desired.

CHEF'S NOTE

■ If you cannot find *super*-firm tofu, you may use *extra*-firm regular tofu (refrigerated tub) and press it before slicing it into "cutlets." See page 11 for instructions on "How to Press Tofu."

OVEN-FRIED TOFU NUGGETS

Makes 4 servings ▪ **Prep Time:** 25 minutes / **Bake Time:** 55 to 70 minutes

Reminiscent of frozen chicken sticks, this enticing finger food recipe makes a delightful entrée to please kiddos *and* grownups!

1 block (15 to 16 ounces) super-firm tofu (refrigerated package or tub, see Chef's Note), drained

2 cups gluten-free cornflakes

2 teaspoons Italian seasoning blend

½ teaspoon smoked paprika

¼ teaspoon salt

2 tablespoons extra-virgin olive oil

¼ cup unsweetened dairy-free milk

Preheat the oven to 375°F. Line a large, rimmed baking sheet with unbleached parchment paper.

Cut the tofu into about 24 "nuggets" or "sticks," each about ½-inch thick.

Put the cornflakes, Italian seasoning, paprika, and salt into a re-sealable plastic bag and crush into coarse crumbs, using your hands or a rolling pin. Transfer the crumbs to a medium-sized bowl. Add the oil and stir with a large spoon to coat the crumbs evenly with the oil.

Pour the dairy-free milk into a small, shallow bowl.

Dip each tofu nugget into the dairy-free milk to generously coat and then dip it into the cornflake crumbs. Press the cornflake crumbs *firmly* onto the tofu nugget. Put the coated tofu nugget on the lined baking sheet. Continue in this manner until all of the tofu nuggets are coated and arranged in a single layer on the baking sheet.

Tent with foil and bake for 30 minutes. Remove the foil and bake for 25 to 40 minutes more or until the coating is very crispy and golden brown. (Baking time *will* vary, depending upon how thickly you have cut your tofu nuggets.) Cool for 5 minutes and serve with *Maple-Mustard Dipping Sauce* (page 101) or *Classic Cocktail Sauce* (page 102) on the side.

CHEF'S NOTE

▪ If you cannot find *super*-firm tofu, you may use *extra*-firm regular tofu (refrigerated tub) and press it before slicing it into "cutlets." See page 11 for instructions on "How to Press Tofu."

PANTRY POLENTA LASAGNA

Makes 4 to 6 servings ▪ **Prep Time:** 20 minutes / **Bake Time:** 65 to 70 minutes

This incredibly flavorful lasagna is quick to assemble using mostly pantry ingredients. With 20 minutes to prepare for the oven and about 1 hour of baking time, you'll be serving your family one of the most delicious Italian-style casseroles you've ever prepared. (No need to tell them it was *so* easy to make!)

SAUCE

1 jar (24 to 26 ounces) vegan marinara sauce or *Easy Marinara Sauce* (page 103)

1 tablespoon extra-virgin olive oil

1 tablespoon gluten-free tamari *or* coconut aminos

2 teaspoons Italian seasoning blend

¼ teaspoon crushed red pepper (use ⅛ teaspoon for less spicy)

VEGAN RICOTTA

1 block (15 to 16 ounces) extra-firm regular tofu (refrigerated tub), drained and broken into chunks (see Chef's Note)

1 tablespoon extra-virgin olive oil

1 tablespoon gluten-free tamari *or* coconut aminos

1 teaspoon Italian seasoning blend

Freshly ground black pepper, to taste

LASAGNA

1 tube (16 to 18 ounces) *very* cold, precooked sun-dried tomato or Italian-style flavored, gluten-free polenta, cut into 24 thin slices (see Chef's Note)

2 cans (4 ounces each) sliced cremini or white button mushrooms, well drained (see Chef's Note)

½ teaspoon Italian seasoning blend

continued on the next page ➤

Preheat the oven to 375°F.

SAUCE

To make the sauce, put all of the sauce ingredients into a medium-sized bowl and stir with a large spoon to combine.

VEGAN RICOTTA

To make the ricotta, put all of the vegan ricotta ingredients into a medium-sized bowl. Mash to the consistency of ricotta cheese using a potato masher or large fork.

LASAGNA ASSEMBLY

Evenly pour one-third of the marinara sauce mixture into the bottom of a 9- x 12-inch (or similarly sized) casserole dish.

Arrange 12 polenta slices in an even layer over the marinara sauce mixture. Top the polenta slices with all of the tofu mixture, spreading it evenly over the polenta slices and gently compressing it with the back of a spoon or spatula. Arrange all of the mushrooms in an even layer over the tofu. Top the mushrooms with one-third of the marinara sauce mixture.

Arrange the remaining 12 polenta slices in an even layer over the marinara sauce layer. Top with the remaining one-third of the marinara sauce mixture, and then sprinkle ½ teaspoon Italian seasoning blend over the marinara sauce.

Cover tightly and bake for 35 minutes. Carefully remove the foil (steam will be *hot!*), tent it *very loosely* over the lasagna, then bake for an additional 30 to 35 minutes or until the top of the casserole becomes slightly golden.

Put the casserole on a wire rack and let cool for 12 to 15 minutes before cutting it into 12 equal sized squares. Serve 2 to 3 squares per person with a simple green salad or steamed green vegetables on the side.

CHEF'S NOTES

■ If preferred, you may use 1½ boxes (16 to 18 ounces) of aseptic packed extra-firm tofu in place of the refrigerated variety. The resulting tofu ricotta will not be as firm, but it will still be quite tasty!

■ If you are cooking gluten-free, be certain to buy certified gluten-free tubes of precooked polenta to ensure that the polenta is completely free of gluten.

■ You may use sliced fresh mushrooms in place of the canned variety, if desired. To do so, sauté 8 ounces of sliced fresh mushrooms in 1 teaspoon of olive oil and/or a bit of water, for about 7 minutes, before adding them to the lasagna.

VEGGIE-LICIOUS QUINOA & TOFU CASSEROLE

Makes 4 servings ■ **Prep Time:** 20 minutes / **Bake Time:** 60 to 70 minutes

This hearty and filling casserole makes a full meal! Featuring lots of veggies, along with protein rich quinoa *and* tofu, this dish makes super easy-to-prepare, casual weeknight fare. Bonus: This is a great way to use leftover cooked quinoa!

2 cups cooked quinoa or *Laura's Easy Quinoa* (page 194)

2 cups cubed zucchini (leave peel on)

2 cups bite-sized broccoli florets

¾ cup diced yellow or sweet onion

½ block (7 to 8 ounces) super-firm *or* extra-firm regular tofu, (refrigerated package or tub), drained and cut into 1- to 1½-inch cubes

1 can (14 to 15 ounces) fire-roasted or plain diced tomatoes, with juice

½ cup water

1 tablespoon extra-virgin olive oil

2 teaspoons Italian seasoning blend

¼ rounded teaspoon crushed red pepper

¼ rounded teaspoon salt

Preheat the oven to 400°F. Put all of the ingredients into a large bowl and gently stir with a large spoon to combine. Transfer to a large casserole dish with tight fitting lid. Bake for 60 to 70 minutes. Cool 10 minutes and serve!

ZUCCHINI LASAGNA
WITH TOFU-KALE RICOTTA

Makes 4 servings ■ **Prep Time:** 30 minutes / **Bake Time:** 55 to 60 minutes

Thinly sliced zucchini stands in beautifully for noodles in this light but satisfying take on the Italian-American classic. Using canned mushrooms helps to cut down on the somewhat lengthy assembly time of this dish, but if you have some extra time, you may use sliced and sautéed fresh mushrooms, in place of the canned variety.

TOFU-KALE RICOTTA

1 block (15 to 16 ounces) extra-firm regular tofu (refrigerated tub), drained

1 tablespoon plus 1 teaspoon extra-virgin olive oil, divided

1 teaspoon Italian seasoning blend

½ teaspoon garlic powder

½ teaspoon salt

Several grinds of black pepper

2½ cups (firmly packed) *very thinly* sliced curly kale, thick stems removed

LASAGNA

2½ cups vegan marinara sauce or *Easy Marinara Sauce* (page 103)

1 tablespoon extra-virgin olive oil, divided

2 to 3 large zucchini, cut lengthwise into 26 to 28 "noodles" (each ⅛- to ¼-inch thick), saving any odd-shaped pieces to top lasagna

¼ teaspoon garlic powder

¾ cup finely diced sweet onion

2 cans (4 ounces each) sliced cremini or white button mushrooms, well drained (see Chef's Note about mushrooms, page 124)

1 teaspoon Italian seasoning blend

continued on page 128 ➤

Zucchini Lasagna,
ready for oven

Preheat the oven to 400°F.

TOFU-KALE RICOTTA

To make the vegan ricotta, put the tofu, 1 tablespoon olive oil, 1 teaspoon Italian seasoning, ½ teaspoon garlic powder, ½ teaspoon salt, and a few grinds of freshly ground pepper into a medium-sized bowl. Mash to the consistency of ricotta cheese using a potato masher or large fork.

Put the kale and 1 teaspoon olive oil in a small bowl and toss with tongs or a fork to coat. Fold the kale into the tofu ricotta mixture.

LASAGNA ASSEMBLY

Spread 1 cup of the marinara sauce evenly in the bottom of a 9- x 12-inch (or similarly sized) casserole dish. Drizzle 1 teaspoon olive oil over the sauce. Arrange about 12 of the zucchini "noodle" slices over the sauce. Drizzle 1 teaspoon olive oil and sprinkle ¼ teaspoon garlic powder over the zucchini slices.

Top the zucchini slices with all of the tofu/kale mixture, spreading it evenly over the zucchini slices and gently compressing it with the back of a spoon or spatula. Spoon ⅔ cup of the marinara sauce evenly over the tofu/kale layer.

Sprinkle all of the diced onions in an even layer over the sauce. Arrange about 12 of the zucchini "noodle" slices on top of the onions.

Arrange all of the mushrooms in an even layer over the zucchini slices. Top the mushrooms with the remaining sauce. Cut the remaining zucchini "noodle" slices and any extra odd-shaped zucchini pieces into strips by slicing them lengthwise into thin strips. Arrange the zucchini strips in a criss-cross pattern over the mushrooms (shown on the previous page).

Drizzle 1 teaspoon olive oil and sprinkle 1 teaspoon Italian seasoning over the top of the lasagna.

Cover with foil and bake 40 to 45 minutes or until bubbling. Carefully remove the foil (steam will be *hot!*), tent it *very loosely* over the lasagna, then bake for about 15 minutes more, or until the top becomes slightly golden brown. Put the casserole on a wire rack and let cool for 15 to 20 minutes. Cut into squares and serve.

EGGPLANT LASAGNA
WITH VEGAN CHIVE RICOTTA

Makes 6 servings ■ **Prep Time:** 35 minutes / **Bake Time:** 65 to 70 minutes

Thinly sliced eggplant stands in for most of the noodles, paired with a layer of polenta "noodle" slices, mushrooms and a flavorful tofu-chive ricotta, making this attractive dish a real showstopper at your supper table. Your family is gonna love it!

VEGAN CHIVE RICOTTA

1 batch *Vegan Chive Ricotta* (page 109)

EGGPLANT

1 medium eggplant, sliced lengthwise into 10 to 12 slices (each about ¼-inch thick)

2 tablespoons extra-virgin olive oil

1 teaspoon Italian seasoning blend

¼ rounded teaspoon garlic powder

LASAGNA

1 jar (24 to 26 ounces) vegan marinara sauce or *Easy Marinara Sauce* (page 103)

1 tablespoon extra-virgin olive oil, divided

2 cans (4 ounces each) sliced cremini or white button mushrooms, well drained (see Chef's Note about mushrooms, page 124)

⅔ tube (about 10 ounces) *very* cold, precooked sun-dried tomato or Italian-style flavored, gluten-free polenta, cut into 6 to 8 thin, *lengthwise* slices (see Chef's Note)

1 teaspoon Italian seasoning blend

Preheat the oven to 400°F. Line a large, rimmed baking sheet with unbleached parchment paper.

VEGAN CHIVE RICOTTA
Prepare one batch of *Vegan Chive Ricotta*.

continued on the next page ▷

EGGPLANT

Arrange the eggplant slices in an even layer on the baking sheet. Brush 2 tablespoons olive oil over the eggplant slices. Sprinkle the eggplant slices with 1 teaspoon Italian seasoning and ¼ rounded teaspoon garlic powder. Bake for 10 to 12 minutes, or until the eggplant slices are beginning to soften.

LASAGNA ASSEMBLY

Put 1 cup vegan marinara sauce and 1 teaspoon olive oil into the bottom of a 9- x 13-inch (or similarly sized) casserole dish and stir to evenly coat the bottom of the dish.

Arrange 5 to 6 eggplant slices in a single layer over the sauce. Spread one-half of the *Vegan Chive Ricotta* in an even layer over the eggplant slices. Spread all of the mushrooms over the vegan ricotta, in an even layer.

Arrange all of the polenta slices in an even layer over the mushrooms and top them with ⅔ cup marinara sauce. Drizzle 2 teaspoons olive oil over the sauce. Spread the remaining *Vegan Chive Ricotta* in an even layer over the sauce and top it with the remaining eggplant slices.

Top with the remaining marinara sauce (about 1 cup), and then sprinkle 1 teaspoon Italian seasoning over the marinara sauce.

Cover tightly with foil and bake for 35 minutes. Carefully remove the foil (steam will be *hot!*), tent it *very loosely* over the lasagna, then bake for 18 to 20 minutes more. Remove the foil completely and bake for 8 to 12 minutes, or until the top of the eggplant slices become golden.

Put the casserole on a wire rack and let cool for 15 minutes before cutting it into large rectangles. Serve with a simple green salad or steamed green vegetable on the side.

CHEF'S NOTE

■ If you are cooking gluten-free, be certain to buy certified gluten-free tubes of precooked polenta to ensure that the polenta is completely free of gluten.

SWEET & SPICY BROCCOLI-CHICKPEA BAKE

Makes 2 to 3 servings ■ **Prep Time:** 15 minutes / **Bake Time:** 35 to 45 minutes

Broccoli and onions are combined with protein-rich chickpeas, then roasted in a tangy sauce, making a simple but satisfying sheet pan supper!

1 large head of broccoli, cut into florets

1 can (15 to 16 ounces) chickpeas (garbanzo beans), drained and rinsed

1 large sweet onion, thickly sliced

4 heaping tablespoons ketchup

2 tablespoons extra-virgin olive oil

2 tablespoons maple syrup

1 teaspoon sriracha-style hot sauce

½ teaspoon garlic powder

½ teaspoon smoked paprika

⅛ teaspoon salt, plus more, to taste

Preheat the oven to 425°F. Line a large, rimmed baking sheet with unbleached parchment paper.

Put the broccoli florets, chickpeas, and onion into a medium-sized bowl.

Put the ketchup, olive oil, maple syrup, hot sauce, garlic powder, smoked paprika, and salt into a small bowl and whisk to combine.

Pour the sauce over the veggies and chickpeas, and gently stir with a large spoon to thoroughly coat the veggies with the sauce.

Arrange the veggies and chickpeas in a slightly overlapping layer on the lined baking sheet (shown on the opposite page). Bake for 35 to 45 minutes, or until the veggies and chickpeas are very tender and the edges have become golden brown. Stir the veggies and chickpeas once (or twice) during baking. Transfer the baking sheet to a wire rack and sprinkle with more salt, to taste, if desired. Cool for 5 minutes and serve over quinoa, rice, or pasta, if desired.

SPAGHETTI SQUASH CASSEROLE

Makes 4 servings ■ **Prep Time:** 10 minutes / **Bake Time:** 60 to 70 minutes

Cooked spaghetti squash takes center stage in this hearty and appealing casserole that's perfect to serve for a satisfying weekday supper. Using leftover squash makes this dish quick to assemble with easy clean up!

CASSEROLE

3 to 3½ cups pre-cooked, cold spaghetti squash "noodles" (recipe for *Baked Spaghetti Squash,* page 220)

1½ cups vegan marinara sauce or *Easy Marinara Sauce* (page 103)

1¼ cups frozen green peas

1 tablespoon extra-virgin olive oil

1 teaspoon Italian seasoning blend

TOPPING

1 cup gluten-free cornflakes, lightly crushed

½ teaspoon Italian seasoning blend

¼ teaspoon salt

1 tablespoon extra-virgin olive oil

CASSEROLE

Preheat the oven to 400°F. Put all of the casserole ingredients into a large bowl and stir with a large spoon to combine. Transfer to a 9- x 12-inch (or similarly sized) casserole dish. Cover and bake for 45 minutes.

TOPPING

Meanwhile, to make the topping, put the crushed cornflakes, ½ teaspoon Italian seasoning, and ¼ teaspoon salt into a small bowl and stir to combine. Add 1 tablespoon olive oil and stir to coat the cornflakes with the oil.

Put the casserole dish on a wire rack. Carefully uncover the casserole (steam will be *very* hot!) and sprinkle the cornflake mixture evenly over the top of the casserole. Bake for an additional 15 to 20 minutes, or until the cornflake topping is crispy.

Transfer the casserole to a wire rack and let cool for about 15 minutes before slicing into rectangles. Serve warm with a crisp green salad or serve with *Steamed Broccoli with Roasted Cashews* (page 207) or *Lemony Broccoli with Sunflower Seeds* (page 208) on the side, if desired.

TEMPEH-VEGGIE BAKE

Makes 3 to 4 servings ▪ **Prep Time:** 17 minutes / **Bake Time:** 45 to 50 minutes

Slow baking tempeh and veggies in a flavorful sauce makes an easy sheet pan supper that will win raves at the dinner table.

SAUCE

¼ cup ketchup

2 tablespoons extra-virgin olive oil

2 tablespoons maple syrup

2 tablespoons gluten-free tamari *or* coconut aminos

1 tablespoon water

1 teaspoon chili powder

TEMPEH & VEGGIES

1 package (8 ounces) tempeh, cut in 1-inch cubes

8 ounces cremini or white button mushrooms, cut in half (or thirds)

8 to 10 mini sweet peppers, seeded and quartered

½ medium-large sweet onion, sliced

Preheat the oven to 400°F. Line a medium-sized, rimmed baking sheet with unbleached parchment paper.

SAUCE

Put the ketchup, olive oil, maple syrup, tamari, water, and chili powder into a small bowl and briskly whisk until combined.

TEMPEH & VEGGIES

Put the tempeh, mushrooms, peppers, and onions into a medium-sized bowl. Add the sauce and stir together using a large spoon until the tempeh and veggies are evenly coated.

ASSEMBLY

Arrange the tempeh and veggies in a single layer on the lined baking sheet. Tent with foil and bake for 30 minutes. Remove the foil and gently stir the tempeh and veggies. Bake uncovered for an additional 15 to 20 minutes or until the tempeh and veggies are golden brown. Cool for 5 minutes and serve with *Quinoa and Peas* (page 189) or *Laura's Easy Quinoa* (page 194), if desired.

BBQ TEMPEH TRIANGLES

Makes 4 servings ■ **Prep Time:** 10 minutes / **Bake Time:** 55 to 70 minutes

A quick and easy BBQ sauce slathered over tender tempeh makes a super flavorful way to serve a protein-packed, plant-based entrée to your family.

1 package (8 ounces) tempeh

⅓ heaping cup ketchup

2 tablespoons water

1 tablespoon maple syrup

1 tablespoon extra-virgin olive oil

½ teaspoon smoked paprika

Preheat the oven to 400°F. Line an 8-inch square, rimmed baking pan with foil and then top the foil with parchment paper.

Cut the brick of tempeh in half to make 2 rectangles. Cut each rectangle *diagonally* into a triangle to make 4 triangles. Turn each triangle on its side and *carefully* slice *it* in half so that you have 2 thinner triangles. Continue in this manner until you have 8 thin tempeh triangles in all. (To be sure the tempeh cooks properly; it is important to have thin tempeh triangles for this.)

Arrange the 8 triangles of tempeh in a single layer on the lined baking pan, cut side facing up.

To make the sauce, put the ketchup, water, maple syrup, olive oil, and smoked paprika into a small bowl and briskly whisk until combined.

Spoon a generous amount of sauce evenly over each tempeh triangle and gently spread it over the tempeh using a rubber spatula or back of a teaspoon. Cover tightly with foil and bake for 30 minutes.

Remove the foil and bake for an additional 25 to 40 minutes or until the tempeh is tender and very browned around the edges. Cool for 5 minutes. Serve with *Roasted Zucchini and Summer Squash Slices* (page 19), *Chili Roasted Broccoli and Mushrooms* (page 205) and *Red Potato Oven Fries* (page 176), if desired (shown on the opposite page).

ROASTED VEGGIE PLATTER

Makes 2 to 3 main dish servings ■ **Prep Time:** 25 minutes / **Bake Time:** 40 to 50 minutes

This colorful veggie plate makes a satisfying meal served with your favorite cooked grain in the center of each plate. This hearty platter is tasty served cold, too!

SQUASH

1 small butternut squash, peeled, cut in half, seeded and sliced into ¼- to ½-inch thick rounds and/or slices

1 tablespoon extra-virgin olive oil

Salt, to taste

Freshly ground black pepper, to taste

PEPPERS

2 medium sweet red or orange bell peppers, seeded and quartered

½ tablespoon extra-virgin olive oil

Salt, to taste

Freshly ground black pepper, to taste

FENNEL

1 large head fennel, root end, tough stalks and fronds removed

1 tablespoon extra-virgin olive oil

1 teaspoon Italian seasoning blend

Salt, to taste

Freshly ground black pepper, to taste

Preheat the oven to 400°F. Line several medium-sized, or one very large, rimmed baking pan(s) with unbleached parchment paper.

SQUASH

Put the squash rounds, 1 tablespoon olive oil, salt, and pepper to taste, into a large bowl and gently toss with a large spoon to combine. Arrange the squash slices in an even layer on a prepared pan.

continued on page 140 ➤

PEPPERS

Put the quartered peppers, ½ table-spoon olive oil, salt, and pepper to taste, into the same large bowl and gently toss with a large spoon to combine. Arrange the peppers in an even layer on a prepared pan.

FENNEL

Cut the fennel bulb into ¼- to ½-inch thick slices. Put the fennel, 1 tablespoon olive oil, 1 teaspoon Italian seasoning, salt, and pepper to taste, into the same large bowl and gently toss with a large spoon to combine. Arrange the fennel slices in an even layer on a prepared pan.

Bake the squash, peppers, and fennel for 35 minutes. Put the pan(s) on a wire rack and flip the veggies over. Bake for an additional 10 to 15 minutes, or until the veggies are soft and starting to brown around the edges. Put the pan(s) on a wire rack and let cool for 5 minutes.

Equally divide and arrange the veggies on two to three large dinner plates or small platters. Put a generous scoop of *Cashew-Scallion Quinoa* (page 194), *Laura's Easy Quinoa* (page 194), or *Flavorful Brown Basmati Rice* (page 190), artfully arranged in the center of the plate and arrange the veggies around the quinoa or rice (shown on the previous page) and serve.

PECAN-CRUSTED ZUCCHINI FILETS

Makes 2 to 3 servings ■ **Prep Time:** 20 minutes / **Bake Time:** 30 to 40 minutes

My husband says these crispy "filets" are a good stand-in for the seafood variety. With a crunchy pecan and cornflake crust coating tender slices of zucchini, then baked until golden brown—I think I might agree!

PECAN TOPPING

½ cup gluten-free cornflakes

⅓ cup pecan halves

1 teaspoon Italian seasoning blend

2 teaspoons extra-virgin olive oil

⅛ teaspoon salt

ZUCCHINI "FILETS"

1 rounded tablespoon Dijon mustard

1 tablespoon maple syrup

1 large zucchini, sliced diagonally into 10 to 14 "filets," each about ¼-inch thick

2 to 3 teaspoons extra-virgin olive oil

Preheat the oven to 425°F. Line a large, rimmed baking sheet with unbleached parchment paper.

PECAN TOPPING

Put the pecan topping ingredients into a blender or food processor and pulse into *coarse* crumbs. Transfer the crumbs to a medium-sized bowl.

ZUCCHINI "FILETS"

Put the mustard and maple syrup into a medium-sized bowl and briskly whisk until combined.

Dip each zucchini slice into the mustard/maple mixture to lightly coat then dip it into the pecan/cornflake crumbs. Gently press the pecan/cornflake crumbs onto the zucchini slice. Put the coated zucchini slice on the lined baking sheet. Continue in this manner until all of the zucchini slices are coated. Drizzle 2 to 3 teaspoons olive oil evenly over the zucchini slices.

Bake for 30 to 40 minutes or until the zucchini "filets" are tender, coating is crispy, and the edges have become golden brown. Cool for 5 minutes and serve with a dipping sauce like *Classic Cocktail Sauce* (page 102) or *Smoky and Spicy Burger Sauce* (page 98) on the side.

Spicy Eggplant Rollatini, ready for oven (page 162)

EASY & ENTICING ENTRÉES

If you are seeking a delectable dish to star in a festive meal, look no further! Here, tofu gets decked out in a flavorful baked dish, stir fry, and sauté, while squash, tempeh, beans, cauliflower, and mushrooms all get their turn to take center stage in these tantalizing and tasty recipes!

HOT CHA-CHA TOFU!

Makes 4 servings ■ **Prep Time:** 12 minutes / **Refrigeration Time:** 45 minutes to 1 hour / **Bake Time:** 60 to 70 minutes

Bathed in a spicy sauce and baked in the oven, this snazzy tofu dish makes a protein-powered, vegan entrée any night of the week. If you are not usually a fan of baked tofu, give this recipe a try—it's jazzylicious!

1 block (15 to 16 ounces) super-firm regular tofu, drained (refrigerated package or tub, see Chef's Note)

2 tablespoons ketchup

2 tablespoons maple syrup

2 tablespoons water

1 tablespoon extra-virgin olive oil

1 teaspoon sriracha-style hot sauce (use ½ teaspoon for less spicy)

Line a 9-inch square baking pan with foil, then line the foil with unbleached parchment paper.

Cut the tofu into 10 thin "cutlets" by first slicing it down the middle to make two halves. Turn each half on its side and slice it into five uniform slices. Repeat with the other half of the tofu block, to make 10 tofu slices in all. Snugly arrange the tofu slices in a single layer in the lined baking pan.

To make the sauce, put the ketchup, maple syrup, water, olive oil, and hot sauce into a small bowl and briskly whisk until combined.

Spoon a scant tablespoon of sauce over each tofu slice and gently spread it over the tofu slice using a rubber spatula or back of a teaspoon. Cover with foil and refrigerate for 45 minutes to 1 hour.

Preheat the oven to 375°F. Bake the tofu (covered) for 30 minutes. Increase the oven temperature to 425°F. Remove the foil and bake for an additional 30 to 40 minutes or until the tofu is crisp and golden brown around the edges. Cool for 5 minutes and serve with *Quinoa and Peas* (page 189) and *Steamed Cauliflower Wedges* (page 216), if desired (shown on the opposite page).

CHEF'S NOTE

■ If you cannot find *super-firm* regular tofu, you may use 1½ blocks (about 24 ounces) *extra-firm regular* tofu (refrigerated tub) and press it for 1 to 3 hours before assembling this recipe. (See page 11 for instructions on "How to Press Tofu.")

BROCCOLI-TOFU SZECHUAN SAUTÉ

Makes 3 to 4 servings ■ **Prep Time:** 20 minutes / **Stove Top:** 24 to 26 minutes

Reminiscent of a specialty dish that my husband and I ordered years ago from our favorite New York Chinese eatery, this recipe makes a great stand-in for the restaurant classic. Sautéed over medium-high and medium heat (rather than quickly fried over high heat), this easy-to-prepare favorite was inspired by the traditional Szechuan version—with a jazzy twist, of course!

BROCCOLI & TOFU

1 block (15 to 16 ounces) super-firm *or* extra-firm regular tofu (refrigerated package or tub), drained and cut into 1-inch cubes (pressing first is not required)

2 teaspoons gluten-free tamari *or* coconut aminos

2 tablespoons extra-virgin olive oil, divided

7 to 8 cups bite-sized broccoli florets

¼ teaspoon crushed red pepper (use ½ teaspoon for extra spicy!)

SMOKY SAUTÉ SAUCE

3 tablespoons maple syrup

2 tablespoons gluten-free tamari *or* coconut aminos

2 tablespoons water

½ teaspoon smoked paprika

½ teaspoon ground turmeric

½ teaspoon garlic powder

BROCCOLI & TOFU

Put the tofu and 2 teaspoons tamari in a medium-sized bowl and gently toss using a large spoon until the tofu is coated with the tamari. Cover and refrigerate for 15 to 30 minutes to allow the tamari to marinate the tofu.

continued on the next page ➤

SMOKY SAUTÉ SAUCE

Meanwhile, put all of the *Smoky Sauté Sauce* ingredients into a small bowl and stir with a whisk to combine. Cover and refrigerate until you are ready to prepare the recipe.

ASSEMBLY

Put the tofu, 1 tablespoon olive oil, and 1 tablespoon of the *Smoky Sauté Sauce* into a large sauté pan. Cover and cook over medium-high heat, stirring occasionally, for 4 minutes. Decrease the heat to medium or medium-low, and add 1 more tablespoon of the *Smoky Sauté Sauce*. Cover and cook, stirring occasionally, for 10 minutes.

Add the broccoli florets, 3 tablespoons of the *Smoky Sauté Sauce*, and 1 more tablespoon oil. Increase the heat to medium-high, cover and cook, stirring occasionally, for 6 to 7 minutes. Add ¼ teaspoon crushed red pepper and the remaining *Smoky Sauté Sauce*. Cover and cook, stirring occasionally, for 3 to 4 minutes or until the broccoli is al dente.

To serve, spoon a generous amount of the Szechuan sauté over *Laura's Easy Quinoa* (page 194), *Cashew-Scallion Quinoa* (page 194), or *Flavorful Brown Basmati Rice* (page 190) and serve immediately.

BOK CHOY, RED PEPPER & TOFU SAUTÉ

Makes 4 to 5 servings ■ **Prep Time:** 25 minutes / **Stove Top:** 31 to 36 minutes

Tender bok choy combined with sweet red peppers and tender tofu makes a lovely meal served over cooked quinoa or rice.

EASY SAUTÉ SAUCE

3 tablespoons maple syrup

1½ tablespoons gluten-free tamari *or* coconut aminos

¼ rounded teaspoon garlic powder

TOFU

1 block (15 to 16 ounces) super-firm *or* extra-firm regular tofu (refrigerated package or tub) drained and cut into 1-inch cubes (see Chef's Note)

1 tablespoon gluten-free tamari *or* coconut aminos

1 tablespoon extra-virgin olive oil

¼ rounded teaspoon garlic powder

¼ teaspoon crushed red pepper (use ½ teaspoon for extra spicy!)

1½ tablespoons *Easy Sauté Sauce*

BOK CHOY & PEPPERS

1 large head bok choy or 6 to 8 small heads baby bok choy, washed well and sliced (see Chef's Note for slicing instructions)

1 large sweet red bell pepper, seeded and sliced

1 tablespoon extra-virgin olive oil

¼ teaspoon crushed red pepper (use ½ teaspoon for extra spicy!)

1 tablespoon gluten-free tamari *or* coconut aminos

EASY SAUTÉ SAUCE

Put all of the *Easy Sauté Sauce* ingredients into a small bowl and stir with a whisk to combine.

continued on the next page ➤

TOFU

Put the tofu, 1 tablespoon tamari, 1 tablespoon oil, ¼ rounded teaspoon garlic powder, and ¼ teaspoon crushed red pepper into a large sauté pan. Cover and cook over medium-high heat, stirring occasionally, for 8 to 10 minutes. Decrease the heat to medium and add 1½ tablespoons of the *Easy Sauté Sauce*. Cover and cook, stirring occasionally, for 6 minutes, or until the tofu is golden brown. Transfer the tofu to a covered plate to stay warm while you cook the veggies.

BOK CHOY & PEPPERS

Put the bok choy *stalks*, red pepper slices, 1 tablespoon oil, and ¼ teaspoon crushed red pepper into the pan. Cover and cook over medium-high heat, stirring occasionally, for 4 to 5 minutes.

Decrease the heat to medium, uncover and cook for 2 minutes, to allow some of the excess moisture (from the bok choy *stalks*) to cook down. Add the bok choy *leaves* and 1 tablespoon tamari, cover and cook, stirring occasionally, for 2 to 3 minutes. Uncover and cook for 2 minutes more, to allow any of the excess moisture to cook down.

Add the tofu back into the pan, along with all of the remaining *Easy Sauté Sauce*. Cover and cook, stirring occasionally, for 5 to 6 minutes or until the tofu is heated through.

To serve, spoon a generous amount of the Szechuan sauté over *Laura's Easy Quinoa* (page 194) *Cashew-Scallion Quinoa* (page 194), or *Flavorful Brown Basmati Rice* (page 190) and serve immediately.

CHEF'S NOTES

■ If you are using extra-firm regular tofu, you must press the tofu first. See instructions for "How to Press Tofu" on Page 11.

■ To cut large bok choy *or* baby bok choy, start by cutting off the tough root end from each head of bok choy. Remove any discolored leaves, separate the stalks, and place in a bowl of water. Swish the stalks to loosen any bits of dirt from the stalks. Put the stalks in a large colander, rinse well under cold running water and then drain. Gather the clean stalks into a bunch, put them on a cutting board and slice the stalks crosswise, starting at the root end. When you get to the tender green leaves, roll them up and cut across into thin slices. At this point, thoroughly rinse the bok choy stalk slices *and* leaves again (in separate colanders) under cold running water, to be certain all of the sand and dirt is *thoroughly* removed.

CHILI ROASTED CAULIFLOWER STEAKS
WITH CRISPY MUSHROOMS

Makes 4 servings ■ **Prep Time:** 30 minutes / **Bake Time:** 50 to 60 minutes / **Stove Top:** 12 to 14 minutes

Tender cauliflower "steaks" are roasted in the oven and served with a crispy mushroom topping. This recipe has several steps, but it's well worth the effort!

CAULIFLOWER STEAKS

2 small heads cauliflower

1 tablespoon extra-virgin olive oil

1 tablespoon plus 1 teaspoon chili pepper infused extra-virgin olive oil (see Chef's Note)

¼ teaspoon garlic powder

¼ teaspoon smoked paprika

¼ teaspoon salt

CRISPY MUSHROOMS

12 ounces sliced cremini or white button mushrooms

1 tablespoon extra-virgin olive oil

1 teaspoon Italian seasoning blend

½ teaspoon garlic powder

¼ teaspoon salt

1 cup crushed gluten-free cornflakes

Water, if needed

Preheat the oven to 400°F. Line a medium-sized, rimmed baking pan with unbleached parchment paper.

CAULIFLOWER STEAKS

Trim about 2 inches off the two opposite sides of each cauliflower head and set aside for another use. Carefully cut each cauliflower head into two ¾- to 1-inch thick "steaks," as if slicing a loaf of bread.

Coat the parchment paper with 1 tablespoon olive oil. Arrange the four cauliflower steaks in a single layer on the parchment paper. Brush each steak with 1 teaspoon of the chili infused oil (see Chef's Note). Evenly sprinkle ¼ teaspoon garlic powder, ¼ teaspoon smoked paprika, and ¼ teaspoon salt over the four cauliflower steaks.

Tent with foil and bake for 30 minutes or until the cauliflower begins to soften. Carefully remove the foil and bake for 20 to 30 minutes more, or until the edges of the cauliflower steaks are golden. Transfer the pan to a wire rack and let cool 5 minutes.

continued on the next page ▷

CRISPY MUSHROOMS

While the cauliflower steaks bake, make the crispy mushrooms. Put the mushrooms, 1 tablespoon oil, Italian seasoning, ½ teaspoon garlic powder, and ¼ teaspoon salt in a sauté pan. Cover and cook, stirring occasionally, for 10 to 12 minutes, or until the mushrooms are soft and starting to brown around the edges. Remove the cover and sprinkle the mushrooms with the crushed cornflakes. Cook for 1 to 2 minutes, stirring often, adding a tiny bit of water or oil if pan becomes dry.

Serve one cauliflower steak per person, with one-quarter of the crispy mushrooms spooned over the top. This dish is nice served with a green salad and *Quinoa and Peas* (page 189) on the side.

CHEF'S NOTE

■ If preferred, you may use plain extra-virgin olive oil in place of the chili-infused variety to coat the cauliflower steaks. Then, sprinkle ⅛ teaspoon chili *powder* over each cauliflower steak before baking. Proceed with recipe as directed.

LAURA'S HEARTY VEGAN MEATLOAF

Makes 6 servings ■ **Prep Time:** 35 minutes / **Bake Time:** 85 to 95 minutes

This easy-to-assemble loaf is delicious, hearty, and appetizing. The white beans and pecans add a meaty texture, while the marinara sauce and spices add flavor. Serve this loaf at any family meal to rave reviews, guaranteed!

1½ cups pecan halves

1 cup plus 2 tablespoons gluten-free, quick cooking rolled oats

1½ rounded cups vegan marinara sauce, divided

1 can (14 to 16 ounces) great northern white beans, drained and rinsed (see Chef's Note)

1½ tablespoons gluten-free tamari or coconut aminos

1 tablespoon Italian seasoning blend

¾ teaspoon garlic powder, divided

2½ teaspoons maple syrup, divided

Preheat the oven to 375°F. Line a 9- x 5-inch loaf pan with unbleached parchment paper, leaving a 2½-inch overhang on the two lengthwise sides of the pan to make paper "wings."

Put the pecans into a blender or food processor and process (on medium *or* low) into *coarse* crumbs. Transfer the pecan crumb mixture to a large bowl. Add the rolled oats and stir with a large spoon to combine.

Put 1 cup marinara sauce, white beans, tamari, Italian seasoning, ½ teaspoon garlic powder, and ½ teaspoon maple syrup into the blender or food processor and process (on medium) into a *very chunky* purée making certain that some chunky pieces of the beans remain. Add the marinara/bean mixture to the pecans and oatmeal and stir with a large spoon to combine.

Spoon the loaf mixture into the prepared pan and smooth the top of the loaf with a spatula, pressing it down in order to compress the loaf. Fold the paper "wings" over the top of the loaf and gently press down with your hands. This will

continued on the next page ➤

help to hold the loaf together while it bakes. Cover the loaf (tightly) with foil.

While the loaf bakes, make the glaze. Put ½ cup marinara sauce, 2 teaspoons maple syrup and ¼ teaspoon garlic powder into a small bowl and stir with a whisk to combine.

Bake the loaf for 45 minutes. Remove the foil and bake for 20 minutes. Put the pan on a wire rack and carefully peel back the parchment paper "wings" that are covering the top of the loaf. Spread the glaze evenly over the top of the loaf. Bake uncovered for an additional 20 to 30 minutes or until the loaf is golden brown around the edges and *very* firm to the touch.

Transfer the pan to a wire rack and let cool for 2 minutes to allow it to firm up slightly. Using the paper "wings," lift the loaf out of the pan and put it on the rack. Let cool 10 to 15 minutes before gently pulling back the paper and slicing. Carefully cut the loaf into 8 to 9 slices, using a serrated bread knife and wiping the knife clean after cutting each slice. Serve the loaf with *Cauliflower, Potato, and Spinach Mash-Up* (page 181) on the side, if desired.

CHEF'S NOTE

■ You may use *any* variety of white beans this recipe.

ROCKIN' BLACK BEAN BURGERS

Makes 7 burgers ■ **Prep Time:** 25 minutes / **Bake Time:** 24 to 34 minutes

Hearty black beans, walnuts, and rolled oats combined with some snazzy spices create a vegan burger that stands front and center for an easy and satisfying family meal.

2 teaspoons extra-virgin olive oil, plus more as needed, to coat pan and measuring cup

1 can (14 to 16 ounces) black beans, drained and rinsed

⅓ cup flavorful tomato sauce or marinara sauce

2 tablespoons ketchup

1 rounded teaspoon smoked paprika

1 teaspoon Italian seasoning blend

½ teaspoon garlic powder

1½ cups walnut halves

½ cup gluten-free, quick cooking rolled oats

Preheat the oven to 375°F. Line a large, rimmed baking sheet with unbleached parchment paper. Lightly coat the parchment paper with 2 teaspoons of olive oil.

Put the beans, tomato or marinara sauce, ketchup, smoked paprika, Italian seasoning, and garlic powder into a medium-sized bowl and coarsely mash using a potato masher or large fork.

Put the walnuts into a blender or food processor and process into coarse crumbs. Add the ground walnuts and oats to the bean mixture and stir with a large spoon until thoroughly combined.

To form a burger, scoop up ⅓ cup of the mixture using a lightly oiled measuring cup. *Firmly* pack the burger mixture into the measuring cup and drop it onto the prepared pan. Gently press the burger using a flat spatula or clean hands to form it into the shape of a burger. Continue in this manner until you have a total of 7 burgers.

Bake the burgers for 14 minutes. Remove the pan from the oven and flip the burgers over. Bake for an additional 10 to 20 minutes (checking *often*) or until the burgers are golden brown on the bottom and around the edges. (Do not overcook, or the burgers will be too dry.)

Transfer the pan to a wire rack and let the burgers cool 5 minutes. Serve over a leafy green salad, or serve on gluten-free burger buns or English muffins, topped with *Smokin' Coleslaw* (page 55) and drizzled with *Smoky and Spicy Burger Sauce* (page 98).

LAURA'S BUDDHA BOWL

Makes 4 servings ▪ **Assembly Time:** 30 minutes

I created this beautiful dinner bowl that's similar to a New York-style whole food veggie plate. This recipe is not only attractive to look at—it's absolutely satisfying and delicious to eat. Bonus: You can serve it hot *or* cold!

1 large bunch kale, thick stems removed and thinly sliced

4 to 6 cups cooked quinoa, *Cashew-Scallion Quinoa* (page 194), or *Laura's Easy Quinoa* (page 194) (see Chef's Note)

2 large baked sweet potatoes, thickly sliced (see Chef's Note)

1 cup shredded or grated carrots (peeling is optional)

BBQ Tempeh Triangles (page 136) (see Chef's Note)

Sweet and Tangy Tahini Dressing (page 97)

4 tablespoons roasted and salted sunflower seeds

Fit a steamer basket into a medium-large saucepan with a tight-fitting lid. Add 2 to 3 inches of water, and then add the sliced kale. Cover and bring to a boil. Steam the kale for 6 to 9 minutes until tender, making certain it retains a vibrant green color (see Chef's Note).

In each of four deep and wide bowls, arrange 1 to 1½ cups cooked quinoa, one-quarter of the steamed kale, one-quarter of the sweet potato slices, one-quarter of the carrots, and one-quarter of the *BBQ Tempeh Triangles* in a pleasing pattern (shown on the opposite page). Drizzle some of the *Sweet and Tangy Tahini Dressing* over the top of the sweet potatoes and kale. Sprinkle 1 tablespoon sunflower seeds over the top. Assemble all four bowls in this manner and serve with any remaining sauce on the side.

CHEF'S NOTES

▪ The sweet potatoes, quinoa, tempeh triangles, and/or kale may be cooked 24 hours in advance, refrigerated, and served cold, if desired.

▪ If preferred, you may substitute your favorite store-bought pre-baked tofu or cooked chickpeas for the *BBQ Tempeh Triangles.*

SPICY EGGPLANT ROLLATINI

Makes 12 to 14 rolls ▪ **Prep Time:** 30 minutes / **Bake Time:** 60 minutes

Classic rollatini features thinly sliced eggplant rolled up around a ricotta cheese filling and baked in a flavorful tomato sauce, but this recipe has a welcome vegan twist. My plant-powered version uses a quick, homemade dairy-free "ricotta" in place of traditional cheese. The result is an appetizing, tasty entrée that rivals the original.

VEGAN CHIVE RICOTTA

1 batch *Vegan Chive Ricotta* (page 109)

EGGPLANT

1 medium eggplant, sliced lengthwise into 12 to 14 slices (each *about* ⅛-inch thick)

2 tablespoons extra-virgin olive oil

1 teaspoon Italian seasoning blend

¼ rounded teaspoon garlic powder

ROLLATINI

2⅓ cups flavorful vegan marinara, pasta sauce or *Easy Marinara Sauce* (page 103), divided

1 tablespoon extra-virgin olive oil

½ teaspoon crushed red pepper (use ¼ teaspoon for less spicy)

½ rounded cup diced red or sweet onion

2 tablespoons chopped chives or scallions, plus more for garnish

Preheat the oven to 400°F. Line a large, rimmed baking sheet with unbleached parchment paper.

VEGAN RICOTTA

Prepare one batch of *Vegan Chive Ricotta*.

EGGPLANT

Arrange the eggplant slices in an even layer on the baking sheet. Brush 2 table-spoons oil over the eggplant slices. Sprinkle the eggplant with 1 teaspoon Italian seasoning and ¼ rounded teaspoon garlic powder. Bake for 10 to 12 minutes, just until the eggplant slices are *beginning* to soften and have become pliable. Do not

continued on page 164 ➤

overcook! Put the baking sheet on a wire rack and let the slices cool for 5 to 10 minutes.

ROLLATINI ASSEMBLY

Put 1 cup vegan marinara sauce and 1 tablespoon olive oil into the bottom of a 9- x 13-inch (or similarly sized) casserole dish and stir with a spoon to evenly coat the bottom of the dish. Sprinkle the crushed red pepper evenly over the sauce. Arrange the diced onion in an even layer over the sauce.

Spoon 2 to 2½ heaping tablespoons of *Vegan Chive Ricotta* onto one end of each eggplant slice. Gently roll the eggplant slice tightly around the *Vegan Chive Ricotta* and place it, seam side down on top of the sauce and onions in the baking dish. Continue in this manner until you have 12 to 14 rolls.

Spoon 1 heaping tablespoon of the remaining marinara sauce over each roll, then sprinkle 2 tablespoons chopped chives or scallions over the rolls (shown on page 142).

Cover tightly and bake for 60 minutes or until the eggplant is very tender. Put the dish on a wire rack and carefully uncover (steam will be *hot!*) Let stand 5 to 7 minutes. Serve 2 to 3 rolls per person arranged over *Laura's Easy Quinoa* (page 194) or *Flavorful Brown Basmati Rice* (page 190), garnished with more chopped chives or scallions.

SPAGHETTI WITH SPICY BASIL-POMODORO SAUCE

Makes 4 to 6 servings ∎ **Prep Time:** 15 minutes / **Stove Top:** 22 to 27 minutes

Here's a quick dish with a real Italian flair. Just a few ingredients are simmered to deliver a full-bodied tomato sauce laced with a pop of garlic and fresh basil, then spooned over gluten-free pasta, for a satisfying weeknight meal.

4 small cloves garlic, minced

1 tablespoon extra-virgin olive oil

¼ teaspoon salt

1 can (about 28 ounces) crushed tomatoes

½ cup water, plus more as needed

½ teaspoon vegan light *or* dark brown sugar (optional)

¼ teaspoon crushed red pepper

1 cup fresh basil, torn into small pieces

12 to 16 ounces gluten-free spaghetti, penne, or your favorite pasta variety

Put the garlic, olive oil, and salt in a large sauté pan and cook over medium heat for 2 minutes, stirring often.

Add the tomatoes, water, sugar, and crushed red pepper. Decrease the heat to medium-low, cover and simmer, stirring occasionally, for 15 minutes. Add the basil, cover and simmer, stirring occasionally, for 5 to 10 minutes.

While the sauce cooks, bring a large pot of salted water to a boil over medium-high heat. Stir in the spaghetti. Decrease the heat to medium-low and cook according to package directions, stirring occasionally, until al dente. Drain the spaghetti.

To serve, equally divide the spaghetti into each of four to six pasta bowls. Ladle the sauce over the top and serve immediately.

FESTIVE STUFFED PEPPERS

Makes 4 servings ■ **Prep Time:** 45 minutes / **Bake Time:** 60 to 70 minutes

My mom often served stuffed peppers for supper when I was a little girl and I always looked forward to those meals. This vegan version of mom's specialty highlights quinoa, pecans, spinach, and other nutritious ingredients to create a tasty entrée that's perfect to serve for a casual supper or celebratory dinner.

4 small sweet bell or green bell peppers, any combination of colors

2 tablespoons plus 1 teaspoon extra-virgin olive oil, divided

¾ teaspoon salt, divided

Freshly ground black pepper, to taste

2 cups cooked *Laura's Easy Quinoa* thoroughly cooled *or* chilled (see Chef's Note)

1 cup (firmly packed) chopped baby spinach

½ cup sliced grape tomatoes

½ cup diced pecans

¼ cup minced red onion

1½ teaspoons Italian seasoning blend

¼ teaspoon garlic powder

Preheat the oven to 375°F. Line a medium-sized casserole dish with unbleached parchment paper making certain that the dish will hold all the peppers snugly so they remain upright during baking.

Slice off the top ⅛- to ¼-inch from each pepper. Seed the peppers. Brush 1 teaspoon of the oil over the outside and inside cavity of each pepper. Sprinkle about ⅛ teaspoon salt and a generous amount of black pepper, to taste, inside the cavity of each pepper.

Put the cooked quinoa, baby spinach, grape tomatoes, pecans, onion, Italian seasoning, garlic powder, and ¼ teaspoon salt into a large bowl and stir until well combined. Add 1 tablespoon olive oil and stir to combine.

Spoon one-fourth of the quinoa mixture into each pepper, pressing it *firmly* into the pepper cavity and mounding it above the top. Arrange the peppers upright in the casserole. Cover and bake for 30 minutes. Increase the oven temperature to 400°F. Continue to bake (covered) for 15 minutes. Uncover the peppers and bake for 15 to 25 minutes more, or until the top of the stuffing is golden and the peppers are tender. Let cool for 10 minutes. For a festive but easy holiday supper, serve *Pumpkin Pie Spiced Butternut Squash Soup* (page 76) for the first course and *Date-Nut Snowballs* for dessert (page 259).

CHEF'S NOTE

■ I like to use tri-color quinoa for this stuffing, but white quinoa is fine too. To save time, *Laura's Easy Quinoa* (page 194) can be cooked and refrigerated up to 24 hours in advance of preparing this recipe.

STUFFED DELICATA SQUASH

Makes 4 servings ■ **Prep Time:** 35 minutes / **Bake Time:** 75 to 90 minutes

Creamy and sweet on the inside with a delicate outer skin, Delicata squash makes a welcome vessel for a savory quinoa stuffing. Pair this easy dish with steamed greens or a simple side salad and you have a hearty and comforting meal. Bonus: This recipe makes great use of leftover quinoa!

SQUASH

2 small Delicata squash (each about 7 to 9 inches in length), sliced in half lengthwise

1 tablespoon plus 1 teaspoon extra-virgin olive oil, divided

Salt, to taste

Freshly ground black pepper, to taste

FILLING

2½ cups cooked *Laura's Easy Quinoa*, thoroughly cooled or chilled (see Chef's Note)

1⅓ cups diced fresh tomatoes

⅔ cup diced walnuts

3 medium scallions, green and white parts, thinly sliced

1 tablespoon extra-virgin olive oil

2 teaspoons Italian seasoning blend

¼ teaspoon salt

Preheat the oven to 400°F. Line a medium-sized, rimmed baking pan with unbleached parchment paper.

SQUASH

Using a grapefruit spoon or sturdy teaspoon, scoop out the seeds from the inside of the squash halves. Season *each* squash half with 1 teaspoon olive oil. Add a liberal amount of salt and pepper to taste.

Arrange the squash halves cut side down on the prepared pan and bake for 25 minutes (see Chef's Note), or until the outside of the squash is soft to the touch and the inside edge of each squash half is golden. Put the pan on a wire rack and let the squash cool for about 20 minutes.

FILLING

While the squash cools, put all of the filling ingredients into a medium-sized bowl and stir with a large spoon to combine.

ASSEMBLY

Once the squash is cool enough to handle, turn each squash half over and fill each half with a generous amount of the quinoa/walnut mixture.

Line a medium-sized casserole dish with unbleached parchment paper. Arrange the stuffed squash halves snugly in the dish, making certain they stand upright. Cover and bake for 35 to 40 minutes. Uncover and bake for an additional 15 to 25 minutes, or until the top of the filling is starting to brown. Transfer the dish to the wire rack and let cool 5 to 7 minutes before serving.

CHEF'S NOTES

- The baking time for the squash will vary depending upon the size of the squash.
- *Laura's Easy Quinoa* (page 194) can be cooked and refrigerated up to 24 hours in advance of preparing this recipe.

SPAGHETTI SQUASH BOWLS

Makes 6 servings ▪ **Prep Time:** 1 hour / **Bake Time:** 70 minutes

These enticing spaghetti bowls are a fun way to serve squash as the main event for a weeknight meal. They are kid-friendly and stand in beautifully for a classic spaghetti dinner.

3 small spaghetti squash (about 6 inches in length), sliced in half lengthwise

2 tablespoons extra-virgin olive oil, divided

Salt, to taste

Freshly ground black pepper, to taste

Chunky Mushroom Marinara Sauce (page 104) or a jarred "chunky-style" vegan marinara sauce

Preheat the oven to 400°F. Line a medium-sized, rimmed baking pan with unbleached parchment paper. Using a grapefruit spoon or sturdy teaspoon, scoop out the seeds and stringy flesh from the inside of each squash. Season each squash half with 1 teaspoon olive oil. Add a liberal amount of salt and pepper to taste.

Arrange the spaghetti squash halves cut side down on the prepared pan and bake for 40 minutes, or until the outside of the squash is slightly soft to the touch. Put the pan on a wire rack and let the squash cool for 10 to 20 minutes.

Once the squash halves are cool enough to handle, turn each squash half over and carefully loosen the spaghetti squash "noodles" away from the skin, but *do not remove the strands* from the squash halves. Take great care to keep the outer skin intact, since this will serve as the "bowls." Top each of the squash "bowls" with a generous amount of *Chunky Mushroom Marinara Sauce* or your preferred "chunky-style" vegan marinara sauce.

Line a deep casserole dish with unbleached parchment paper. Carefully arrange the filled squash halves snugly in the dish, making certain they stand upright. Cover tightly and bake for 15 minutes. Uncover and bake for an additional 15 minutes. Transfer the dish to a wire rack and let cool 5 to 7 minutes before serving.

SPICY BAKED PORTOBELLO MUSHROOMS
WITH GARLIC AND CAPERS

Makes 4 to 6 servings ■ **Prep Time:** 15 minutes / **Bake Time:** 40 to 45 minutes

Serve these mushroom giants as a main event with a cooked grain and steamed green veggies on the side—or serve 'em in a bun (like a burger) topped with *Smokin' Coleslaw* (page 55) and *Smoky and Spicy Burger Sauce* (page 98).

6 Portobello mushrooms, stems removed

1 tablespoon gluten-free tamari *or* coconut aminos

1 tablespoon water

1 large clove garlic, minced

1 teaspoon Dijon mustard

⅛ teaspoon cayenne pepper

2 tablespoons non-pareil capers, drained and rinsed

Preheat the oven to 400°F. Line a large, rimmed baking sheet with unbleached parchment paper.

Arrange the mushrooms, gill sides up, on the lined baking sheet.

To make the sauce, put the tamari, water, garlic, Dijon, and cayenne pepper in a small bowl and stir with a whisk to combine. Add the capers and gently stir to combine.

Drizzle one-sixth of the sauce evenly over the gills of each mushroom. Tent with foil and bake for 40 to 45 minutes or until the mushrooms are very soft. Serve in burger buns with classic toppings, or serve with *Flavorful Brown Basmati Rice* (page 190) and *Easy Green Beans with Vegan Butter Sauce* (page 202) on the side, if desired.

Red Potato Oven Fries
(page 176)

SNAZZY SPUDS & GREAT GRAINS

Everybody loves spuds! Potatoes, along with rice, quinoa, and polenta are breakfast, lunch and supper staples. These crowd-pleasing recipes are filling, nutritious, and delicious, making an excellent side dish for any wholesome family meal.

RED POTATO OVEN FRIES

Makes 3 to 4 servings ■ **Prep Time:** 10 minutes / **Bake Time:** 45 to 55 minutes

If you like fries, these babies are sure to please, and baking them in the oven makes them easy and delicious. Using red potatoes with the peel on assures great texture, better nutrition, and taste. Serve 'em with a burger, salad, or sandwich and you're good to go!

6 to 7 medium/large
   red potatoes

1½ tablespoons extra-virgin
   olive oil

1 rounded teaspoon Italian
   seasoning blend

¼ teaspoon salt, plus
   more to taste

Several generous grinds of
   black pepper

Preheat the oven to 400°F. Line a medium-sized, rimmed baking sheet with unbleached parchment paper.

Cut each potato into 8 thick wedges. Put the potatoes, olive oil, Italian seasoning, and salt into a mixing bowl and stir with a large spoon to coat. Add several generous grinds of black pepper and stir to combine.

Arrange the potatoes in an even layer on the prepared pan. Bake for 45 to 55 minutes, or until the potatoes are golden and crisp. Taste and add more salt, if desired. Let cool 5 minutes and serve.

HOT N' SPICY BABY POTATOES

Makes 4 to 6 servings ■ **Prep Time:** 7 minutes / **Bake Time:** 45 to 50 minutes

If you like hot and spicy food this recipe is for you. *But*—if you *don't* like hot and spicy food this recipe is for you, too, because you can simply leave out the cayenne pepper and still have a flavorful spud side dish.

1½ pounds baby Dutch yellow or baby red potatoes, scrubbed

1 tablespoon extra-virgin olive oil

1 teaspoon smoked paprika

¼ teaspoon garlic powder

¼ teaspoon salt

⅛ teaspoon cayenne pepper

Preheat the oven to 400°F. Line a medium-sized, rimmed baking sheet with unbleached parchment paper.

Put the potatoes and olive oil in a mixing bowl and stir with a large spoon to coat.

Put the smoked paprika, garlic powder, salt, and cayenne pepper into a small bowl and stir with a small whisk or spoon to combine. Sprinkle the spice mixture over the potatoes and stir to thoroughly coat.

Arrange the potatoes in an even layer on the prepared pan. Bake for 45 to 50 minutes, or until the potatoes are golden. Cool 5 minutes and serve.

CAULIFLOWER, POTATO & SPINACH MASH-UP

Makes 4 to 6 servings ■ **Prep Time:** 12 minutes / **Stove Top:** 15 to 20 minutes

This substantial side dish is a fun way to change up mashed spuds, and it's a great way to sneak cauliflower *and* spinach into your family's meals!

3½ to 4 cups cubed white, red, or yellow potatoes, (1-inch cubes, peeling is optional)

3½ to 4 cups cauliflower florets (cut into small florets)

1 cup water, plus more as needed

½ large (or 1 small) vegan gluten-free bouillon cube, crumbled

3½ to 4 cups (lightly packed) baby spinach

2 teaspoons vegan buttery spread

Salt, to taste

Freshly ground black pepper, to taste

Put the potatoes and cauliflower florets into a medium-sized saucepan. Add 1 cup water and the crumbled bouillon cube. Cover and bring to a boil over medium-high heat. Decrease the heat to medium-low, cover and cook for 10 to 15 minutes, or until the potatoes and cauliflower florets are *almost* soft, checking often and adding an additional ¼ cup water if the pan starts to become dry.

Add the spinach, cover and cook for 5 minutes, or until the potatoes and cauliflower florets are soft and the spinach is wilted. Remove the pan from the heat and add the vegan buttery spread. Using a potato masher, mash all of the veggies together with the bouillon broth that is still in the bottom of the pan, making certain to incorporate the spinach into the potatoes and cauliflower mixture. Season with salt and pepper to taste, and serve.

EASY TWICE BAKED SPUDS

Makes 4 servings ■ **Prep Time:** 10 minutes / **Bake Time:** 30 to 40 minutes

These yummy, easy-to-prepare, steak-style oven "fries" make a great use of leftover baked potatoes. Feel free to change up the seasonings to create a special spud side dish to suit your family's tastes.

4 large baked russet potatoes, well chilled (see Chef's Note)

1½ tablespoons extra-virgin olive oil

1 teaspoon Italian seasoning blend (see Chef's Note)

Salt, to taste

Freshly ground black pepper, to taste

Preheat the oven to 400°F. Line a medium-sized, rimmed baking sheet with unbleached parchment paper.

Cut each potato into 6 to 8 thick wedges. Put the potatoes, olive oil, Italian seasoning, salt and pepper in a medium-sized bowl and *gently* toss with a large spoon to coat.

Arrange the potatoes in an even layer on the prepared pan. Bake for 30 to 40 minutes, or until the outside of each potato "steak fry" is golden and crispy. Cool 3 to 5 minutes and serve.

CHEF'S NOTES

■ You may bake, cool, and refrigerate the potatoes up to 2 days before assembling this recipe.

■ For a different taste, you may use 1 teaspoon of smoked paprika *or* chili powder in place of the Italian seasoning, if desired.

MASHED RED POTATOES
WITH SCALLIONS

Makes 4 to 6 servings ■ **Prep Time:** 15 minutes / **Stove Top:** 17 to 20 minutes

Here's a flavorful and festive way to serve red potatoes. A generous addition of chopped fresh scallions gives these creamy spuds a jazzed-up twist!

6 to 6½ cups cubed red potatoes with peel (cut in 1-inch cubes)

1 cup water, plus more as needed

½ large (or 1 small) vegan gluten-free bouillon cube, crumbled

⅔ cup chopped scallions (I like to use white *and* green parts)

1 tablespoon vegan buttery spread

Salt, to taste

Freshly ground black pepper, to taste

Put the potatoes into a medium-sized saucepan. Add 1 cup water and the crumbled bouillon cube. Cover and bring to a boil over medium-high heat. Decrease the heat to medium-low, cover and cook for 12 minutes, checking often and adding an additional ¼ cup water, if the pan starts to become dry.

Add the chopped scallions, cover and cook for 5 minutes more, or until the potatoes are very soft. Remove the pan from the heat and add the vegan buttery spread. Using a potato masher, mash the potatoes and scallions together with the bouillon broth that is still in the bottom of the pan. Season with salt and pepper to taste and serve.

COLORFUL SWEET & SAVORY POTATO ROAST

Makes 4 servings ∎ **Prep Time:** 10 minutes / **Bake Time:** 45 to 55 minutes

Here's a different way to offer a substantial side dish for a casual meal. This winning combination of potatoes is pleasing to the palate and attractive to serve!

2 medium sweet potatoes, cut into thick, ½-inch slices or wedges (leave peels on)

6 to 8 white fingerling or small white potatoes, cut into ½-inch thick rounds (leave peels on)

2 tablespoons extra-virgin olive oil

1 teaspoon Italian seasoning blend

¼ teaspoon salt, plus more to taste

Preheat the oven to 375°F. Line a medium-sized, rimmed baking sheet with unbleached parchment paper.

Put the potatoes, olive oil, Italian seasoning, and salt in a medium-sized bowl and toss with a large spoon to coat.

Arrange the potatoes in an even layer on the prepared pan. Cover with foil and bake for 20 minutes. Remove the foil and bake for an additional 25 to 35 minutes or until the undersides of the potatoes are golden and crispy. Put the pan on a wire rack and season with more salt to taste and serve.

STEAMED SWEET POTATOES
WITH MAPLE SYRUP GLAZE

Makes 4 to 6 servings ■ **Prep Time:** 15 minutes / **Stove Top:** 20 to 30 minutes

This flavorful sweet potato dish is very easy to prepare. It's hearty, pleasingly sweet and totally delicious! This is an excellent side dish to serve for a family supper or holiday meal.

4 very large (or 5 to 6 medium) sweet potatoes, peeled and cubed

2 tablespoons maple syrup, plus more as needed

2 teaspoons vegan buttery spread (optional)

¼ teaspoon ground cinnamon, plus more for serving

Fit a steamer basket into a large pot with a tight fitting lid. Add 2 to 3 inches of cold water, then add the sweet potatoes. Cover, bring to a boil and steam for 20 to 30 minutes, or until the sweet potatoes are soft but not mushy.

Transfer the steamed sweet potato cubes to a medium-sized bowl. Add the maple syrup, optional vegan buttery spread, and cinnamon, and gently stir to coat the cubes. Sprinkle the sweet potatoes with more cinnamon, if desired and serve.

TRI-COLOR QUINOA
WITH BLACK BEANS

Makes 3 to 4 servings ■ **Prep Time:** 10 minutes / **Stove Top:** 17 to 20 minutes

This very quick, protein-packed dish makes a simple but satisfying centerpiece for a weeknight meal, served with a salad or steamed green vegetable on the side. This dish also plays double duty as a hearty side for a more substantial meal.

1 cup uncooked tri-color or white quinoa, rinsed thoroughly

1 can (15 to 16 ounces) black beans, drained and rinsed

1 large vegan gluten-free bouillon cube, crumbled

½ teaspoon chili powder

⅛ teaspoon cayenne pepper

2 cups plus 2 tablespoons water

Put all of the ingredients, in the order listed, into a medium-sized saucepan and stir to combine.

Cover the saucepan and bring to a simmer over medium-high heat. Decrease the heat to medium-low, cover and cook, stirring occasionally, for 17 to 20 minutes, or until most of the water has been absorbed.

Remove the pan from the heat and fluff the quinoa with a fork. Cover and let stand for 5 to 10 minutes before serving.

SERVING SUGGESTION

■ For a festive presentation, divide the quinoa onto three to four plates and top with sliced avocados and tomatoes, if desired (shown on the opposite page).

QUINOA & PEAS

Makes 3 to 4 servings ■ **Prep Time:** 5 minutes / **Stove Top:** 15 to 18 minutes

A pop of green from protein rich green peas combined with the plant-protein powerhouse, quinoa, makes a nutritious and satisfying side dish for a vegan meal.

1 cup uncooked white quinoa, rinsed thoroughly

2¼ cups water

½ large (or 1 small) vegan gluten-free bouillon cube, crumbled

1 cup frozen peas

½ tablespoon vegan buttery spread

Put the quinoa, water, and crumbled bouillon cube into a medium-sized saucepan. Cover and bring to a simmer over medium-high heat. Decrease the heat to medium-low, cover and cook for 8 minutes. Add the frozen peas, cover and cook for 7 to 10 minutes, or until the water is absorbed and peas are heated through.

Remove the pan from the heat and fluff the quinoa with a fork. Add the vegan buttery spread and fluff again. Cover and let stand for 5 to 10 minutes before serving.

VARIATION

■ **Quick Quinoa and Mushrooms:** Replace the frozen peas with 1 can (4 ounces) sliced cremini or white button mushrooms, drained. Proceed with recipe as directed.

FLAVORFUL BROWN BASMATI RICE

Makes 4 servings ■ **Prep Time:** 5 minutes / **Stove Top:** 40 to 45 minutes

Basmati rice has a pleasing aroma and nutty taste that sets it apart from traditional brown rice. I like this method of cooking it because it's easy to prepare, but *very* flavorful!

1 cup brown basmati rice, rinsed thoroughly

2¼ cups water

½ large (or 1 small) vegan gluten-free bouillon cube, crumbled

Put all of the ingredients into a medium-sized saucepan. Cover and bring to a boil over medium-high heat. Decrease the heat to medium-low and simmer for 40 to 45 minutes, or until all of the water is absorbed. Stir with a fork to fluff. Cover and remove from heat. Let the rice stand for at least 10 minutes, or up to 25 minutes before serving. Fluff again and serve.

POLENTA COTTAGE FRIES

Makes 4 servings ■ **Prep Time:** 10 minutes / **Bake Time:** 25 to 35 minutes

When I lived in Manhattan, I liked to order the potato cottage fries at a corner coffee shop. Traditional cottage fries are potatoes that have been sliced into thin rounds and then fried. Here, I have changed it up by using a convenient, precooked tube of Italian herb seasoned polenta in place of the potatoes. Plus, these yummy bites are baked instead of fried. The result is a delicious side dish that even the kiddos will love!

1 tablespoon extra-virgin olive oil, divided

1 tube (16 to 18 ounces) *very* cold, precooked Italian-style flavored (or plain), gluten-free polenta, cut into 20 to 24 slices (see Chef's Note)

Salt, to taste

Freshly ground black pepper, to taste

Preheat the oven to 400°F. Line a large, rimmed baking sheet with unbleached parchment paper.

Brush the parchment with 1½ teaspoons oil. Arrange the polenta slices in an even layer on the prepared pan. Brush the remaining 1½ teaspoons oil over the top of the polenta slices and sprinkle with salt and pepper, to taste.

Bake for 25 to 35 minutes or until the outside of the polenta slices are golden and crispy. Put the sheet on a wire rack and let cool 3 to 5 minutes. Serve with ketchup or *Smoky and Spicy Burger Sauce* (page 98) on the side.

CHEF'S NOTE

■ If you are cooking gluten-free, be certain to buy certified gluten-free tubes of precooked polenta to ensure that the polenta is completely free of gluten.

LAURA'S EASY QUINOA

Makes 3 to 4 servings ■ **Prep Time:** 5 minutes / **Stove Top:** 15 to 18 minutes

This basic recipe is a "must-have" in any plant-powered kitchen.

1 cup uncooked white or tri-color quinoa, rinsed thoroughly

2¼ cups water

½ large (or 1 small) vegan gluten-free bouillon cube, crumbled

Put all of the ingredients into a medium-sized saucepan. Cover and bring to a simmer over medium-high heat. Decrease the heat to medium-low, cover and cook for 15 to 18 minutes, or until all of the water is absorbed.

Remove the quinoa from heat, uncover and gently fluff with a fork. Cover and let stand for 5 to 10 minutes before serving. Stored tightly covered in the refrigerator, cooked quinoa will keep up to 3 days.

VARIATIONS

■ **Cashew-Scallion Quinoa:** Once the quinoa has cooked for 12 minutes, uncover and stir in ½ cup chopped, roasted, and salted cashews and ⅓ cup thinly sliced scallions *or* chives. Cover and simmer for 5 to 7 minutes more, or until all of the water is absorbed and the quinoa is soft. Remove the pan from the heat and stir in ½ tablespoon vegan buttery spread (optional). Cover and let stand for 5 to 10 minutes before serving.

■ **Turmeric Quinoa:** Add ½ teaspoon ground turmeric to the saucepan with all of the other ingredients. Proceed with recipe as directed (shown on the opposite page).

Smoky Summer Squash Slices
(page 198)

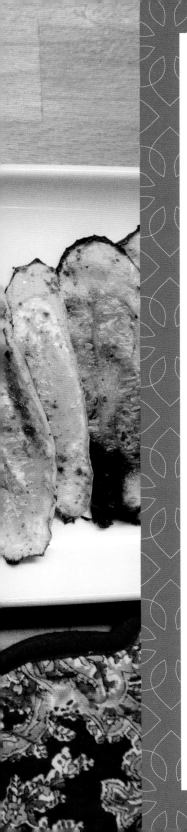

EAT YOUR VEGGIES, PLEASE

OK, let's face it—Mom was right! It's good to eat plenty of vegetables. In this chapter, I take "ho-hum" veggies and transform them into colorful culinary combinations to please even the veggie evaders in your family. These veggie-licious dishes are all easy to prepare, too!

Now, *that's* jazzy.

ROASTED ZUCCHINI SLICES

Makes 2 to 3 servings ■ **Prep Time:** 20 minutes / **Bake Time:** 30 to 40 minutes

Farm-fresh zucchini tossed with a few flavorings and roasted in the oven makes for a simple side dish for an easy supper.

2 medium zucchini, each sliced into 10 to 12 diagonal slices

1½ tablespoons extra-virgin olive oil

1 teaspoon garlic powder

Salt, to taste

Freshly ground black pepper, to taste

Preheat the oven to 400°F. Line a large, rimmed baking sheet with unbleached parchment paper.

Put the zucchini slices, olive oil, and garlic powder into a large bowl. Gently toss with a large spoon to thoroughly coat the slices with the oil and garlic powder. Arrange the zucchini slices in a single layer on the lined baking sheet. Sprinkle the zucchini with a generous amount of salt and pepper, to taste.

Bake for 30 to 40 minutes or until the zucchini slices are very golden and slightly crisp. Cool for 3 to 5 minutes and serve.

VARIATIONS

■ **Smoky Summer Squash Slices**: Replace the zucchini with 2 medium summer squash. Replace the garlic powder with smoked paprika. Proceed with recipe as directed (shown on page 196).

■ **Baked Butternut Squash Slices**: Replace the zucchini with 1 medium butternut squash, peeled, seeded and cut into ½- to ¾-inch thick slices. Omit the garlic powder. Bake for 45 to 55 minutes, or until the squash slices are very tender and the edges are golden brown, flipping the slices halfway through baking. Cool for 3 to 5 minutes and serve.

GARLICKY ROASTED GREEN PEPPERS

Makes 4 servings ■ **Prep Time:** 7 minutes / **Bake Time:** 25 to 40 minutes

Here's an easy and flavorful way to serve fresh green peppers. Roasting them in the oven with a bit of garlic powder really brings out the sweetness from the peppers, making a wholesome side dish for a plant-powered meal.

2 very large (or 3 medium) green peppers

1 tablespoon plus 1 teaspoon extra-virgin olive oil

½ teaspoon garlic powder

Salt, to taste

Freshly ground black pepper, to taste

Preheat the oven to 400°F. Line a medium-sized, rimmed baking sheet with unbleached parchment paper.

Remove the seeds from the peppers and cut each pepper into 8 thick slices. Put the pepper slices, olive oil, garlic powder, salt, and pepper into a medium-sized bowl and toss using a large spoon until the pepper slices are evenly coated.

Arrange the pepper slices in a single layer, skin side down, on the lined baking sheet. Bake for 25 to 40 minutes, or until soft and the bottoms of the peppers are very brown. Cool for 5 minutes and serve.

EASY GREEN BEANS
WITH VEGAN BUTTER SAUCE

Makes 3 to 4 servings ■ **Prep Time:** 15 minutes / **Stove Top:** 7 to 9 minutes

Fresh green beans are lightly steamed and drizzled with vegan butter to create a kiddo-friendly veggie side.

12 ounces green beans, washed and trimmed

1 heaping tablespoon vegan buttery spread

Salt, to taste

Freshly ground black pepper, to taste (optional)

Fit a steamer basket into a medium-large saucepan with a tight-fitting lid. Add 2 to 3 inches of water, and then add the green beans. Cover and bring to a boil. Steam the beans for 7 to 9 minutes or until crisp tender.

Transfer the beans to a large bowl. Add the vegan buttery spread and gently stir to thoroughly coat the beans. Top with salt and several grinds of optional black pepper to taste and serve.

CHILI ROASTED BROCCOLI & MUSHROOMS

Makes 3 to 4 servings ∎ **Prep Time:** 10 minutes / **Bake Time:** 35 to 40 minutes

Roasting broccoli and mushrooms with a bit of chili powder results in a zesty side dish that pairs well with quinoa or rice.

1 very large or 2 small heads of broccoli, cut into large florets

8 ounces cremini mushrooms, sliced in half (about ½-inch thick slices)

2 tablespoons extra-virgin olive oil

1 tablespoon chili-infused olive oil (see Chef's Note)

1 rounded teaspoon chili powder

¼ teaspoon salt, plus more to taste

Preheat the oven to 400°F. Line a large, rimmed baking sheet with unbleached parchment paper.

Put the broccoli florets, mushrooms, olive oil, and chili-infused olive oil into a medium-sized bowl and toss using a large spoon to combine. Sprinkle with the chili powder and salt and mix together using a large spoon until the broccoli and mushrooms are evenly coated.

Arrange the broccoli and mushrooms in a single layer on the lined baking sheet. Bake for 35 to 40 minutes or until the broccoli and mushrooms are very tender and the edges have become golden brown. Cool for 5 minutes and serve.

CHEF'S NOTE

∎ If desired, you may use plain extra-virgin olive oil in place of the chili-infused olive oil.

PAPRIKA SEASONED ZUCCHINI "FRIES"

Makes 2 to 3 servings ▪ **Prep Time:** 10 minutes / **Bake Time:** 25 to 30 minutes

Cutting julienne-style zucchini sticks, adding a few seasonings and then baking them in the oven creates a "fry-like" side dish that your family will truly appreciate!

2 medium zucchini, each cut into 8 to 10 "sticks"

1 tablespoon extra-virgin olive oil

1 teaspoon smoked paprika

Salt, to taste

Freshly ground black pepper, to taste

Preheat the oven to 400°F. Line a medium-sized, rimmed baking sheet with unbleached parchment paper.

Put all of the ingredients in a medium-sized bowl and gently toss with a large spoon to coat.

Arrange the zucchini sticks in an even layer on the prepared pan. Bake for 25 to 30 minutes or until the outside of the zucchini sticks are golden. Cool 3 to 5 minutes and serve.

STEAMED BROCCOLI
WITH ROASTED CASHEWS

Makes 4 to 6 servings ■ **Prep Time:** 10 minutes / **Stove Top:** 7 to 9 minutes

Roasted and salted cashews add *crunch*, while a sweet and tangy sauce adds *punch* to this delightful broccoli dish.

6 cups (about 1 pound) broccoli florets

1 tablespoon extra-virgin olive oil

1 tablespoon maple syrup

1 tablespoon gluten-free tamari *or* coconut aminos

¼ rounded teaspoon smoked paprika

⅓ cup roasted and salted cashews

Freshly ground black pepper, to taste

Fit a steamer basket into a medium-large saucepan with a tight-fitting lid. Add 2 to 3 inches of water, and then add the broccoli florets. Cover and bring to a boil. Steam the broccoli florets for 7 to 9 minutes or until tender.

While the florets steam, make the sauce. Put the olive oil, maple syrup, tamari, and smoked paprika into a small bowl and whisk until combined.

Transfer the florets to a large bowl. Sprinkle the cashews over the broccoli florets. Add the sauce and gently stir to thoroughly coat the florets with the sauce. Top with several grinds of black pepper to taste and serve.

LEMONY BROCCOLI
WITH SUNFLOWER SEEDS

Makes 4 to 6 servings ▪ **Prep Time:** 10 minutes / **Stove Top:** 7 to 9 minutes

Lively and lemony with a little bit of crunch from roasted sunflower seeds, this recipe makes an appetizing way to serve broccoli as a welcome side dish.

6 cups (about 1 pound) broccoli florets

1 tablespoon vegan buttery spread

1½ tablespoons freshly squeezed lemon juice

2 tablespoons roasted and salted sunflower seeds

Salt, to taste

Freshly ground black pepper, to taste

Fit a steamer basket into a medium-large saucepan with a tight-fitting lid. Add 2 to 3 inches of water, and then add the broccoli florets. Cover and bring to a boil. Steam the broccoli florets for 7 to 9 minutes or until tender.

Transfer the florets to a large bowl. Add the vegan buttery spread and gently stir to coat the florets. Drizzle the florets with the lemon juice and stir to combine. Add the sunflower seeds, salt and pepper to taste and stir again. Serve at once.

SMOKY RAINBOW CARROTS

Makes 3 to 4 servings ■ **Prep Time:** 10 minutes / **Bake Time:** 30 to 40 minutes

A rainbow of hues highlights this simple way to prepare colorful carrots.

5 to 7 medium-large rainbow or orange carrots, peeled (optional) and cut into thick strips

½ tablespoon extra-virgin olive oil

½ teaspoon smoked paprika

Salt, to taste

Freshly ground black pepper, to taste

Preheat the oven to 400°F. Line a medium-sized, rimmed baking sheet with unbleached parchment paper.

Put the carrots, olive oil, smoked paprika, and a generous amount of salt and pepper (to taste) into a medium-sized bowl and toss using a large spoon until the carrots are evenly coated.

Arrange the carrots in a single layer on the lined baking sheet (shown on the opposite page). Bake for 30 to 40 minutes or until the carrots are tender and edges have become golden brown. Cool for 5 minutes and serve.

ROASTED ASPARAGUS
WITH SWEET ORANGE PEPPERS

Makes 4 servings ■ **Prep Time:** 12 minutes / **Bake Time:** 6 to 8 minutes

This dish is an attractive and delicious way to serve fresh asparagus at any family meal.

---

1 pound asparagus, tough stems removed

1 medium sweet orange or red bell pepper, seeded and diced

2 teaspoons extra-virgin olive oil

½ teaspoon garlic powder

½ teaspoon smoked paprika

⅛ teaspoon salt, plus more to taste

Preheat the oven to 375°F. Line a large, rimmed baking sheet with unbleached parchment paper.

Put all of the ingredients into a large bowl and toss with a large spoon to combine.

Arrange the asparagus and peppers in an even layer on the baking sheet (shown on the opposite page). Bake for 6 to 8 minutes or until the asparagus is tender and the peppers are soft. Taste and add more salt, if desired. Serve warm, or cover and refrigerate for 6 hours (or overnight) and serve as a cold side salad.

CORN ON THE COB
WITH BASIL-CHIVE "BUTTER"

Makes 4 servings ■ **Prep Time:** 15 minutes / **Stove Top:** 6 to 7 minutes

This summer favorite is made extra-flavorful slathered with an herb infused "butter." For a kid-friendly version, serve the corn with *plain* vegan buttery spread, sans the herbs.

4 medium ears corn on the cob, husks removed, washed, and well-scrubbed

2 tablespoons slightly softened vegan buttery spread

½ tablespoon (firmly packed) minced fresh basil

½ tablespoon (firmly packed) minced fresh chives

Salt, to taste (optional)

Freshly ground black pepper, to taste (optional)

Put the corn in a large pot and add water to cover the corn by about ½ inch. Cover and bring to a boil. Decrease the heat to medium-low and cook for 3 to 4 minutes or until crisp tender. Remove the pot from the heat and let stand for 3 minutes.

While the corn cooks, make the *Basil-Chive "Butter."* Put the vegan buttery spread, basil, and chives into a small bowl and stir vigorously with a dinner fork until combined. Divide the herbed "butter" into four small ramekins.

Transfer the corn to serving plates and let cool for 3 minutes. Put a ramekin of "butter" on each plate. Serve warm with salt and black pepper offered on the side.

STEAMED CAULIFLOWER WEDGES

Makes 4 servings ■ **Prep Time:** 15 minutes / **Stove Top:** 25 to 35 minutes

This is my husband's favorite way to eat cauliflower. Lucky for me, because it's super easy to prepare!

1 medium head cauliflower, cut into 4 wedges

1 heaping tablespoon plus 1 teaspoon vegan buttery spread

Salt, to taste

Several grinds of black pepper

Fit a steamer basket into a large pot with a tight-fitting lid. Add 2 to 3 inches of cold water, then add the cauliflower wedges, making certain they remain upright in the steamer basket. Cover, bring to a boil and steam for about 25 minutes, or until the cauliflower wedges are soft but *not* mushy.

Transfer the cauliflower wedges to a medium-sized bowl. Drizzle 1 heaping teaspoon vegan buttery spread over each wedge. Sprinkle each wedge with a generous amount of salt and pepper, to taste. *Steamed Cauliflower Wedges* are delicious served (shown on the opposite page) with *Hot Cha-Cha Tofu!* (page 144) with *Quinoa and Peas* (page 189).

BUFFALO CAULIFLOWER FLORETS

Makes 4 servings ■ **Prep Time:** 25 minutes / **Bake Time:** 45 to 50 minutes

These flavorful florets are briefly steamed, tossed with snazzy seasonings, and roasted to caramelized perfection.

1 medium head cauliflower, cut into large florets

5 tablespoons ketchup

2 tablespoons maple syrup

1 tablespoon extra-virgin olive oil

¼ rounded teaspoon smoked paprika

Pinch (about ⅟₁₆ teaspoon) cayenne pepper (use ⅛ teaspoon for spicier cauliflower)

Preheat the oven to 400°F. Line a large, rimmed baking sheet with unbleached parchment paper.

Fit a steamer basket into a large pot with a tight-fitting lid. Add 2 to 3 inches of cold water, and then add the cauliflower florets. Steam the cauliflower for 6 to 8 minutes or until *just* al dente. Transfer the florets to a large bowl and let cool 10 minutes.

While the cauliflower cools, put the ketchup, maple syrup, olive oil, smoked paprika, and cayenne pepper into a small bowl and stir with a small whisk to combine.

Pour the ketchup/olive oil mixture over the cauliflower florets and stir together using a large spoon until the florets are completely coated with the ketchup/olive oil mixture.

Arrange the cauliflower florets in a single layer on the prepared pan. Bake for 45 to 50 minutes, tossing once, until the edges of the cauliflower are very brown and caramelized. Put the pan on a wire rack and let the cauliflower cool for 5 minutes. Serve (shown on the opposite page) with *Quinoa and Peas* (page 189) and *Baked Butternut Squash Slices* (page 198).

BAKED SPAGHETTI SQUASH

Makes 4 servings ▪ **Prep Time:** 7 minutes / **Bake Time:** 45 to 55 minutes

Versatile spaghetti squash is a wonderful way to serve a gluten-free "pasta" meal. From stuffed squash to oven-baked casseroles to spaghetti-style dishes, this recipe will come in handy for preparing Italian inspired meals—sans the pasta!

1 medium or large spaghetti squash, sliced in half lengthwise

2 teaspoons extra-virgin olive oil, divided

Salt, to taste

Freshly ground black pepper, to taste

Preheat the oven to 400°F. Line a medium-sized, rimmed baking pan with unbleached parchment paper.

Using a grapefruit spoon or sturdy teaspoon, scoop out the seeds and stringy flesh from the inside of the squash. Season each squash half with 1 teaspoon olive oil. Add a liberal amount of salt and pepper to taste.

Arrange the spaghetti squash halves cut side down on the prepared pan and bake for 45 minutes to 55 minutes (see Chef's Note), or until the outside of the squash is *very* soft to the touch and the inside edge of each squash half is golden. Put the pan on a wire rack and let the squash cool for about 20 minutes.

When the outside of the squash is cool to the touch, turn the squash upright (see Chef's Note). Scoop out the spaghetti squash strands, breaking them up with a fork to resemble cooked spaghetti. Arrange the strands on individual serving plates and serve with your favorite pasta sauce or *Chunky Mushroom Marinara Sauce* (page 104, shown on the opposite page). Alternately, the squash is now ready to refrigerate until well chilled to use in *Spaghetti Squash Casserole* (page 134).

CHEF'S NOTE

▪ The baking time for the squash will vary depending upon the size of the squash.

Coconut-Chocolate Chip Quick Cake (page 230)

COOKIES, CAKES, CRISPS & CRUMBLES

We all need a little bit of sweet every now and then, and these confections provide a scrumptious vegan take on several classic desserts. From snazzy cakes to fruit-filled crumbles to chocolate chip cookies, these tasty treats provide a welcome finish to any family meal.

LITTLE BANANA-NUT LOAF CAKES

Makes 12 servings ▪ **Prep Time:** 20 minutes / **Bake Time:** 52 to 58 minutes

These petite treats are sweet and moist and they get their zing from a touch of freshly squeezed citrus juice! The cakes are baked in loaf pans and serve double duty as a tasty dessert, or a delectable quick bread to offer on the side with soup or salad. Any way you serve 'em, they are totally jazzylicious!

CAKES

- ⅓ cup plus 2 tablespoons extra-virgin olive oil, plus more for coating pans, divided
- ½ cup unsweetened dairy-free milk
- 2 tablespoons freshly squeezed lemon juice
- 2⅔ cups gluten-free quick cooking rolled oats
- 2½ teaspoons baking powder
- 1 teaspoon ground cinnamon
- ¼ teaspoon salt
- 1 cup (*very* firmly packed) vegan dark brown sugar
- 1½ cups mashed ripe bananas (about 3 to 3½ medium-sized bananas)
- 1¼ cups chopped walnuts

TOPPING

- 2 tablespoons quick cooking rolled oats, divided
- ¼ scant teaspoon ground cinnamon, divided

Preheat the oven to 350°F. Lightly coat the bottom and sides of two 8- x 4-inch loaf pans with olive oil.

Put the dairy-free milk and lemon juice into a small pitcher and stir with a small whisk to combine. Let stand for 5 to 10 minutes while preparing the batter.

Put 2⅔ cups rolled oats into a blender and process into coarse flour. Put the oat flour into a large bowl. Add the baking powder, cinnamon, and salt and stir with a dry whisk to combine. Add the brown sugar and stir with the whisk to incorporate.

Make a well in the center of the dry ingredients and add the dairy-free milk mixture and ⅓ cup plus 2 tablespoons olive oil. Stir with a large spoon to combine. Fold in the mashed bananas and walnuts.

Divide the batter evenly between the prepared loaf pans and sprinkle 1 tablespoon rolled oats and a scant ⅛ teaspoon ground cinnamon over the top of each loaf cake.

Bake for 40 minutes. Decrease the heat to 325°F and bake for 12 to 18 minutes more, or until the edges of each cake are *very* golden and a toothpick inserted into the center of each cake comes out clean.

Transfer the pans to a wire rack and gently run a table knife around the perimeter of each cake to loosen it from the sides of the pan. Let cool for 30 minutes and carefully (cakes will still be quite soft) invert each cake onto the wire rack. Carefully turn each cake right side up and let cool for an additional 10 to 20 minutes before slicing. Stored in an airtight container in the refrigerator, the cakes will keep for about 3 days.

LEMONY LIME PECAN CAKE

Makes 8 servings ■ **Prep Time:** 12 minutes / **Bake Time:** 45 to 52 minutes

This totally tasty and moist cake is enhanced with a refreshingly zingy lemon-lime flavor. It makes a wonderful afternoon snack or a perfect treat to accompany a cup of coffee or tea.

⅓ cup extra-virgin olive oil, plus more to coat pan

1 cup sweetened *or* unsweetened, plain *or* vanilla flavored dairy-free milk

⅓ cup freshly squeezed lemon juice (zest before squeezing)

2 tablespoons freshly squeezed lime juice

2½ cups freshly ground, gluten-free oat flour (see Chef's Note; see "How to Make Oat Flour," page 27)

1 cup plus 1 tablespoon vegan cane sugar, divided

1 tablespoon lemon zest

2¼ teaspoons baking powder

¼ teaspoon salt

1½ cups pecan halves, coarsely chopped, plus 24 halves to top cake

6 tablespoons water, plus more if needed

Preheat the oven to 375°F. Generously coat a 9-inch square rimmed baking pan with olive oil.

Put the dairy-free milk, lemon juice, and lime juice into a pitcher or bowl and let stand for 5 to 10 minutes. Add ⅓ cup olive oil and stir to combine.

Put the flour, 1 cup sugar, lemon zest, baking powder, and salt into a large bowl and mix with a dry whisk until well combined. Add the chopped pecans and stir to combine. Add the dairy-free milk/olive oil mixture and 6 tablespoons water and mix with a large spoon until incorporated. (If batter still seems a bit dry, add 1 more tablespoon water.)

Transfer the batter into the prepared pan. Arrange 24 pecan halves artfully over the top of the cake and sprinkle the top of the batter with 1 tablespoon of sugar.

Bake for 35 minutes. Decrease the heat to 350°F and bake for an additional 10 to 17 minutes, or until the top is slightly crisp, firm to the touch, and the edges are golden. Put the pan on a wire rack and gently run a table knife around the perimeter of the cake. Let cool for 15 to 20 minutes before slicing and serving. Tightly wrapped and stored in the refrigerator, leftover cake will keep for 3 days.

BANANA-DATE SNACK CAKE

Makes 8 servings ■ **Prep Time:** 20 minutes / **Bake Time:** 45 to 55 minutes

Need a sweet snack cake that doubles as a tasty dessert? This super moist and totally delicious delight features ripe bananas in place of eggs and plump dates to add texture and to replace some of the cane sugar. Serve this satisfying treat paired with herbal tea or a glass of cold dairy-free milk.

⅓ cup plus 1 teaspoon extra-virgin olive oil, divided

2 cups lightly packed pre-ground *or* freshly ground, gluten-free oat flour, plus more if needed (see "How to Make Oat Flour," page 27)

½ cup plus 2 tablespoons vegan cane sugar

1½ teaspoons baking powder

¼ teaspoon salt

⅔ cup pitted and diced Medjool dates

2 medium/large ripe bananas, mashed

¾ cup plus 3 tablespoons sweetened, plain dairy-free milk

1 teaspoon vanilla extract

Preheat the oven to 350°F. Lightly coat a 9-inch square cake pan with 1 teaspoon olive oil.

Put the flour, sugar, baking powder, and salt into a large bowl and stir with a dry whisk until combined. Add the diced dates and stir to combine.

Make a well in the center of the dry ingredients. Add the mashed bananas, dairy-free milk, and vanilla and stir with a large spoon to combine. If the batter seems a bit loose, add 2 to 3 more tablespoons oat flour. Pour the batter into the prepared cake pan.

Bake for 45 to 55 minutes, or until a toothpick inserted into the center of the cake comes out clean. Transfer the pan to a wire rack and gently run a table knife around the perimeter of the cake. Let cool for at least 30 minutes before cutting into squares and serving. Cake will be quite soft while still warm. Stored tightly covered in the refrigerator, leftover cake will keep for about 2 days.

COCONUT-CHOCOLATE CHIP QUICK CAKE

Makes 8 to 10 servings ■ **Prep Time:** 20 minutes / **Bake Time:** 45 to 50 minutes

I love chocolate, I love bananas, and I love coconut, too. Bake 'em together and you get a delicious dessert or snack treat that's easy to make anytime!

¼ cup plus 1 teaspoon extra-virgin olive oil, divided

2⅔ cups freshly ground, gluten-free oat flour (see "How to Make Oat Flour," page 27)

⅔ cup unsweetened shredded dried coconut

⅔ cup vegan cane sugar

2½ teaspoons baking powder

⅛ teaspoon salt

1½ cups unsweetened plain dairy-free milk

¾ rounded cup (*very* firmly packed) mashed ripe bananas (about 1¾ medium-sized bananas)

2 teaspoons vanilla extract

⅔ cup vegan chocolate chips (55% to 70% cacao) (see Variation)

Sliced fresh strawberries, for garnish (optional)

Preheat the oven to 375°F. Lightly coat a 9-inch round cake pan with 1 teaspoon olive oil.

Put the flour, coconut, sugar, baking powder, and salt into a large bowl and stir with a dry whisk to combine. Add the dairy-free milk, mashed bananas, ¼ cup olive oil, and vanilla and stir together using a large spoon until incorporated. Fold in the chocolate chips.

Pour the batter into the prepared pan. Bake for 45 to 50 minutes, or until a toothpick inserted in the center of the cake comes out clean.

Put the pan on a wire rack and gently run a table knife around the perimeter of the cake. Let cool for 30 minutes and carefully invert the cake onto the wire rack. Carefully turn the cake right side up and transfer it to a pretty serving platter. Garnish with sliced fresh strawberries (shown on the opposite page), if desired, then slice and serve. Covered tightly and stored in the refrigerator, leftover cake will keep for about 2 days.

VARIATION

■ **Coconut-Raisin Quick Cake:** Replace the chocolate chips with an equal amount of raisins. Proceed as directed.

PETITE APPLE RAMEKINS
WITH COCONUT-OAT CRUNCH

Makes 4 servings ■ **Prep Time:** 20 minutes / **Bake Time:** 35 minutes

These little apple crisps make a sweet finish to any fall-themed menu. Tender apple slices mixed with a bit of cinnamon, sugar, and maple syrup are topped with a simple combination of ingredients, producing a healthy and delicious dessert. Bonus: This dish makes a great breakfast treat, too!

1 heaping tablespoon vegan buttery spread, plus more for coating ramekins

2 medium/large red apples, cored and thinly sliced (do not peel)

3 heaping tablespoons vegan dark brown sugar, or your favorite dry sweetener, divided

2 tablespoons plus 1 teaspoon maple syrup, divided

½ teaspoon ground cinnamon

½ cup gluten-free, quick cooking *or* old fashioned rolled oats

3 tablespoons unsweetened shredded dried coconut

Preheat the oven to 400°F. Lightly coat four 6-ounce (or similarly sized) oven-safe ramekins with vegan buttery spread.

Put the apples, 1 heaping tablespoon sugar, 1 tablespoon maple syrup, and cinnamon, into a medium-sized bowl. Stir with a large spoon until combined. Divide the apple mixture evenly among the prepared ramekins.

Put the oats, coconut, 1 heaping tablespoon vegan buttery spread, and 2 heaping tablespoons sugar in the same medium-sized bowl. Mix together using your hands or a dough blender until thoroughly incorporated. Sprinkle one-quarter of the oat mixture evenly over the apples in each ramekin.

Put the ramekins in an 8- x 8-inch (or similarly sized) rimmed baking pan. Tent with foil and bake for 30 minutes. Remove the foil and bake for an additional 5 minutes or until the tops are crispy and slightly golden.

Put the pan on a wire rack and let the ramekins cool for 15 to 20 minutes. Drizzle the top of each ramekin with 1 teaspoon maple syrup while they are still warm. Serve warm, or cover and refrigerate, and serve cold. Covered tightly and stored in the refrigerator, leftover apple ramekins will keep for about 2 days.

PEAR & CRANBERRY CRISP

Makes 4 to 6 servings ■ **Prep Time:** 15 minutes / **Bake Time:** 42 to 47 minutes

This autumn-inspired crisp highlights ripe pears combined with tangy dried cranberries, making a wonderful dessert for a weeknight meal. It serves double duty as a comforting breakfast dish or afternoon snack.

¼ cup plus 1 rounded teaspoon vegan buttery spread, plus more as needed, divided

8 small (or 4 to 5 large) ripe Bosc pears and/or D'Anjou pears, cored and sliced (leave peel on)

½ cup sweetened dried cranberries

6 tablespoons vegan dark brown sugar or your preferred dry sweetener, divided

1½ teaspoons ground cinnamon, divided

2¼ cups gluten free, old fashioned *or* quick cooking rolled oats, divided

½ cup unsweetened shredded dried coconut

3 tablespoons maple syrup

Preheat the oven to 375°F. Lightly coat a medium-sized casserole with 1 rounded teaspoon vegan buttery spread.

Put the pears, cranberries, 3 tablespoons brown sugar, and 1 teaspoon ground cinnamon, into a medium-sized bowl, and toss gently to coat. Transfer the pear mixture to the prepared casserole and spread in an even layer.

Put ¾ cup of the rolled oats into a blender or food processor and process into a fine textured oat flour.

Put 1½ cups rolled oats, coconut, freshly ground oat flour, and ½ teaspoon ground cinnamon into a medium-sized bowl. Stir to combine. Add ¼ cup vegan buttery spread, maple syrup, and 3 tablespoons brown sugar. Mix well, using a dough blender or clean hands, until the vegan buttery spread is incorporated. Add a bit more vegan butter, if the topping still seems dry. Scatter the oat topping over the pear mixture and lightly press it into an even layer.

Cover and bake for 30 minutes. Uncover and bake for an additional 12 to 17 minutes, or until the pear crisp is bubbling and golden brown on top. Put the pan on a wire rack and let cool at least 15 minutes before serving.

VARIATION

■ **Pear, Apple, and Cranberry Crisp:** Replace half of the small pears with 4 small or 3 large apples, cored and sliced. Proceed as directed (shown above).

MAPLE, OAT & BANANA P.B. COOKIES

Makes 20 to 24 cookies ■ **Prep Time:** 15 minutes / **Bake Time:** 15 to 20 minutes

These cute little gems are not-too-sweet, but they're *packed* with plenty of flavor. Serve them for a breakfast treat, snazzy snack, or dandy dessert for a healthy cookie any time of day!

1 very large ripe banana, peeled

3 heaping tablespoons chunky *or* smooth peanut butter

2 tablespoons maple syrup

1 cup gluten-free, old fashioned *or* quick cooking rolled oats

⅓ cup unsweetened shredded dried coconut

⅓ cup sweetened dried cranberries *or* raisins

Preheat the oven 375°F. Line a large, rimmed baking sheet with unbleached parchment paper.

Put the banana, peanut butter, and maple syrup into a large bowl and mash into a chunky purée using a potato masher or large fork. Add the oats and coconut and stir with a large spoon to combine. Fold in the cranberries or raisins.

Spoon 1 heaping tablespoon of the oat mixture into the prepared baking sheet and flatten it slightly. Continue in this manner with the remaining oat mixture.

Bake for 15 to 20 minutes, or until the cookies are slightly golden around the edges. Transfer the cookies to a wire rack and let cool 10 to 15 minutes. Stored in an airtight container in the refrigerator, the cookies will keep for about 3 days.

LOVELY LITTLE CHOCOLATE CHIP COOKIES

Makes 16 to 18 cookies ▪ **Prep Time:** 20 minutes / **Bake Time:** 18 to 20 minutes

These petite, semi-sweet cookies feature vegan chocolate chips and oats paired with mashed ripe bananas, maple syrup, and a bit of vegan buttery spread. Here's a delicious, jazzy twist on the All-American cookie classic!

1 cup thinly sliced, very ripe bananas (about 1½ large bananas or 2 medium-sized bananas)

2 tablespoons vegan buttery spread

2 tablespoons maple syrup

1½ cups gluten-free, quick cooking rolled oats

¼ teaspoon baking soda

1⁄16 teaspoon salt

½ cup vegan chocolate chips (50% to 60% cacao)

Preheat the oven to 350°F. Line a large, rimmed baking sheet with unbleached parchment paper.

Put the sliced bananas, vegan buttery spread, and maple syrup into a medium-sized bowl and mash together using a potato masher or large fork until well-combined and only small flecks of the vegan buttery spread are visible.

Put the oats, baking soda, and salt into a large bowl and stir with a dry whisk until combined.

Add the banana/maple syrup mixture to the dry ingredients and stir together using a large spoon until the dough comes together. Fold in the chocolate chips.

Drop 1 heaping tablespoon of the dough onto the lined cookie sheet, spacing the cookies about half an inch apart. Gently flatten the top of each cookie *slightly* with a flat spatula. Bake for 18 to 20 minutes or until the bottom of the cookies are slightly golden, but the tops are still a nice blonde color. Remove the sheet from the oven and transfer the cookies to a wire rack. Cool for 15 minutes before serving. Stored in a tightly covered container in the refrigerator, leftover cookies will keep for 3 days.

BLUEBERRY, OATMEAL & WALNUT SNACK BARS

Makes 10 to 12 bars ■ **Prep Time:** 15 minutes / **Bake Time:** 30 to 40 minutes

Whip up these semi-sweet snack bars in a flash using only six simple ingredients. Perfect to serve for an easy dessert or early morning treat, these scrumptious treats are good for you, too!

3 medium very
   ripe bananas

3 tablespoons maple syrup

½ tablespoon vanilla extract

2 cups gluten-free, quick
   cooking *or* old fashioned
   rolled oats

½ cup chopped walnuts

1 rounded cup fresh
   blueberries

Preheat the oven to 375°F. Line an 8-inch or 9-inch square baking pan with unbleached parchment paper, leaving 3- to 4-inch "wings" on two opposite sides of the pan.

Put the bananas, maple syrup, and vanilla into a medium-sized bowl and mash with a potato masher or large fork into a chunky purée. Add the oats and walnuts and stir with a large spoon to combine. Gently fold in the blueberries.

Spread the dough in an even layer in the prepared pan and smooth out the top with a rubber spatula. Score the dough into 10 to 12 bars using a table knife. Bake for 30 to 40 minutes, or until the bars are firm to the touch and the edges are becoming golden.

Put the pan on a wire rack. Using the parchment paper "wings" as handles, carefully lift the bars out of the pan in one piece. Transfer to a wire rack and let cool for 15 minutes. Again, using the parchment paper "wings" as handles, transfer the bars to a cutting board and carefully cut into 10 to 12 individual bars, using a serrated knife. Stored in an airtight container in the refrigerator, the bars will keep for 2 days.

*Maple-Espresso
Chocolate Mousse
(page 244)*

HAPPY DANCE DESSERTS

Let's celebrate with dazzling desserts! This chapter stars the best creamy puddings, perfect pies, tempting truffles, and velvety toppings that are all so luscious, your family will not believe their taste buds when you tell them: "Yep, they're all vegan *and* gluten-free!"

MAPLE-ESPRESSO CHOCOLATE MOUSSE

Makes 4 to 8 servings ■ **Prep Time:** 10 minutes / **Refrigeration Time:** 4 hours to overnight

Need a decadent tasting chocolaty, dairy and egg-free pudding? This grown-up, not-too-sweet, coffee, maple, and vanilla-laced mousse is super creamy and smooth, designed to please all of the chocolate *and* coffee fans at your table! *Wow.*

¼ cup sweetened *or* unsweetened vanilla flavored dairy-free milk

⅓ cup strong brewed coffee or espresso (see Chef's Note)

3 tablespoons maple syrup

¾ block (about 12 ounces) extra-firm regular tofu (refrigerated tub), drained and crumbled

1 cup vegan chocolate chips (55% to 60% cacao)

Vegan Tangerine Whipped Cream Topping (optional, page 262)

Heat the dairy-free milk, brewed coffee, and maple syrup, in a small saucepan over medium-low heat until simmering hot.

Put the tofu in a high-performance blending appliance. Add the chocolate chips. Pour in the simmering dairy-free milk mixture and process for 30 seconds to 1 minute, or until *completely* smooth. Spoon the mixture into four medium-sized dessert dishes or eight espresso cups, and refrigerate for 4 to 24 hours. Serve chilled with a generous dollop of optional *Vegan Tangerine Whipped Cream Topping* spooned on top.

CHEF'S NOTE

■ For a kid friendly version of this mousse, add an additional ⅓ cup sweetened dairy-free milk and omit the coffee.

VEGAN VANILLA-CHOCOLATE PUDDING

Makes 6 servings ■ **Prep Time:** 10 minutes / **Refrigeration Time:** 4 hours to overnight

This cream-a-licious pudding balances the melodious flavors of vanilla *and* chocolate to make an absolutely rich and delightful dessert. No one will ever know there are only five simple ingredients and no dairy in this smooth and luscious dessert—unless you tell them!

½ cup sweetened vanilla flavored dairy-free milk

3 tablespoons maple syrup

½ block (7 to 8 ounces) extra-firm regular tofu (refrigerated tub), drained and crumbled

1 teaspoon vanilla extract

1 bar (3.5 ounces) sweetened vegan dark chocolate bar (55% to 60% cacao), finely chopped (snack bar, *not unsweetened* baking chocolate)

Heat the dairy-free milk and maple syrup in a small saucepan over medium-low heat until simmering hot.

Put the tofu and vanilla in a high-performance blending appliance. Add the chopped chocolate. Pour in the simmering dairy-free milk mixture and process for 30 seconds to 1 minute, or until *completely* smooth. Pipe or spoon the mixture into six small dessert cups and refrigerate for 4 to 24 hours. Serve chilled.

ORANGE CREAMY, DREAMY PIE
WITH CHOCOLATE CHIP COOKIE CRUMB CRUST

Makes 8 servings ■ **Prep Time:** 30 minutes / **Bake Time:** 40 to 50 minutes

Orange juice provides zing to this cashew cream based pie that's cradled in a thick, crisp, chocolaty cookie crumb crust. This delightful dessert has several steps, but it will dazzle kiddos and adults alike!

CRUST

⅓ scant cup vegan buttery spread, plus more for coating pan

2 cups vegan and gluten-free chocolate chip cookie crumbs (see Chef's Note)

FILLING

1 cup raw cashews (soaked, drained, and rinsed, see Chef's Note)

1 block (14 to 16 ounces) extra-firm regular tofu (refrigerated tub), drained and crumbled

½ cup freshly squeezed orange juice

2 tablespoons gluten-free quick cooking *or* old fashioned rolled oats

1 cup vegan cane sugar

Preheat the oven to 375°F. Generously coat a 9-inch round pie pan with vegan buttery spread.

CRUST

To make the crust, put the cookie crumbs in a medium-sized bowl and add ⅓ scant cup vegan buttery spread. Blend together using a dough blender or clean hands, until the mixture resembles wet sand.

Firmly press the cookie crumb mixture into the bottom and up the sides of the pie pan, using the base of a measuring cup to make certain that the crust is evenly distributed. Crust will be very thick. Bake the crust for 5 minutes. Put the crust on a wire rack. (If the crust has puffed up a bit while par-baking, gently press it flat using the base of the measuring cup again.) Let the crust cool for 10 minutes.

FILLING

To make the filling, put the soaked and drained cashews, tofu, orange juice, oats, and sugar in a blender container. Process for 30 seconds to 1 minute, or until *completely* smooth, stopping once

continued on page 250 ➤

or twice to scrape down the sides of the blender container, if needed.

ASSEMBLY

Pour the filling into the crust. Smooth out the top of the pie filling. Put the pie on a sheet pan and bake for 35 to 45 minutes or until the pie is firm around the sides and *almost* set in the middle. If the edges of the crust are becoming overly brown during baking, tent the crust with small strips of foil during the final 10 to 12 minutes of baking.

Put the pie on a wire rack and let cool for 30 minutes to 1 hour before serving. Or, alternately, let the pie cool for 1 hour, loosely cover with plastic wrap, and refrigerate for 5 to 6 hours and serve cold.

Serve with *Vanilla-Orange "Cream" Date Caramel* (page 261) drizzled over the top, if desired. Covered and stored in the refrigerator, leftover pie will keep for 3 days.

CHEF'S NOTES

■ To make the cookie crumbs, put your favorite store bought chocolate chip cookies or homemade *Lovely Little Chocolate Chip Cookies* (page 238) into a blender or food processor and process (on low) into coarse crumbs.

■ To soak the cashews, put the raw cashews and ½ cup water into a small bowl. Cover and refrigerate for 1 to 4 hours. Drain the cashews and rinse thoroughly in cold water. Proceed as directed.

PEANUT BUTTER & CHOCOLATE PUDDING-PIE

Makes 12 servings ▪ **Prep Time:** 30 minutes / **Refrigeration Time:** 4 hours to overnight

Part pie, part cake, and part creamy, chocolaty pudding, this superb treat will please all of the chocolate *and* peanut butter fans in your life. This luscious recipe has quite a few steps, but the impressive presentation offers a gratifying dessert experience!

CRUST LAYER

1¼ cups vegan and gluten-free chocolate chip cookie crumbs (see Chef's Note)

¼ cup melted vegan buttery spread

PUDDING LAYER

2 aseptic packages (12.3 ounces each) silken extra-firm tofu

⅓ cup vegan dark brown sugar

4 tablespoons natural peanut butter, divided (see Chef's Note)

1½ rounded cups vegan chocolate chips (55% to 70% cacao)

½ cup dairy-free milk (your preferred variety, chocolate flavored is nice)

CRUST LAYER

To make the crust, put the cookie crumbs and melted vegan buttery spread into a medium-sized bowl. Blend together using a dough blender or clean hands, until the mixture resembles wet sand.

Transfer the cookie crumb mixture into a 9-inch square *or* 9-inch round springform pan. Firmly press the cookie crumb mixture into the bottom of the pan, using the base of a measuring cup to make certain that the crust is evenly distributed. Freeze the crust for 10 minutes.

PUDDING LAYER

To make the pudding layer, put the tofu, sugar, and 3 tablespoons peanut butter into a blender or food processor and process until very smooth and creamy. Transfer ½ cup of the tofu/peanut butter mixture into a small bowl. Add 1 additional tablespoon peanut butter to the bowl and briskly whisk to combine. Reserve for swirling into the top of the pie.

continued on page 253 ➤

Add the chocolate chips to the remaining tofu mixture that is still *in* the blender container.

Pour the dairy-free milk into a small saucepan and bring it to a simmer over medium-low heat. Immediately pour the simmering dairy-free milk over the chocolate chips and process for 30 seconds to 1 minute, or until *completely* smooth.

Pour the chocolate/tofu mixture into the partially chilled crust. Drop 6 to 7 spoonfuls of the reserved tofu/peanut butter mixture onto the top of the pie. Then, using a wooden skewer or the tip of a knife, gently swirl the tofu/peanut butter mixture into the top of the pie in a pleasing, marbleized pattern. Refrigerate for 4 to 6 hours.

Once the pie is thoroughly chilled, gently run a table knife around the perimeter of the pie. Carefully release the side of the springform pan to unmold the pie. The pudding layer will be *very* soft and *very* creamy, and the crust will be crunchy. Slice into small wedges or squares and serve on pretty dessert plates with a dessert *spoon* on the side.

CHEF'S NOTES

■ To make the cookie crumbs, put your favorite store bought chocolate chip cookies or homemade *Lovely Little Chocolate Chip Cookies* (page 238) into a blender or food processor and process (on low) into coarse crumbs.

■ If preferred, you may use almond, cashew, hazelnut, or sunflower seed butter in place of the peanut butter.

PUMPKIN-PECAN PIE

Makes 8 to 10 servings ▪ **Prep Time:** 25 minutes / **Bake Time:** 70 to 80 minutes

This rich-tasting pie makes the quintessential dessert for a winter holiday supper. Using pecans in the crust *and* to garnish the top of the pie gives this classic dessert a jazzy twist.

CRUST

⅓ cup vegan buttery spread, plus more to coat pan

¾ cup pecan halves

1 cup gluten-free, quick cooking rolled oats

¼ cup vegan cane sugar

¼ teaspoon pumpkin pie spice

FILLING

1½ blocks (22 to 24 ounces) extra-firm regular tofu (refrigerated tub) drained and crumbled

1 can (15 to 16 ounces) unsweetened pumpkin purée

⅔ cup vegan cane sugar

2 tablespoons maple syrup

1½ teaspoons pumpkin pie spice

¼ teaspoon salt

TOPPING

26 to 30 pecan halves or *Candied Spiced Pecans* (page 256)

Preheat the oven to 350°F. Liberally coat a 9-inch round springform pan with vegan buttery spread.

CRUST

To make the crust, put the pecans in a blender or food processor and process into coarse crumbs. Transfer the pecan crumbs to a medium-sized bowl. Add the rolled oats, ¼ cup sugar, and ¼ teaspoon pumpkin pie spice and stir with a dry whisk to combine. Add ⅓ cup vegan buttery spread and blend together using a dough blender or clean hands, until the mixture resembles wet sand. Firmly press the cookie crumb mixture into the bottom of the springform pan, using the base of a measuring cup to help compress the crust into a flat, even layer. Bake the crust for 10 minutes. Remove the crust from the oven and let cool for 10 to 15 minutes.

FILLING

To make the filling, put the tofu, pumpkin purée, ⅔ cup sugar, maple syrup, 1½ teaspoons pumpkin pie spice, and salt into a blender or food processor and process until smooth and creamy.

ASSEMBLY & TOPPING

Pour the filling into the crust and bake for 40 minutes. Decrease the heat to 325°F and bake for an additional 20 to 30 minutes, or until the center of the filling is firm to the touch. Remove the pan from the oven and place it on a wire rack.

Artfully arrange 26 to 30 pecan halves or *Candied Spiced Pecans* (page 256) on top of the pie in a pleasing pattern (shown below). Cool for 15 minutes, then carefully run a table knife around the perimeter of the pie to ensure it does not stick to the side of the pan. Cool for 15 minutes more.

Release the side of the springform pan to unmold. Cover the pie very loosely and refrigerate for 4 to 24 hours before serving. Serve with *Vegan Whipped Cream Topping* (page 262) on the side, if desired. Covered tightly and stored in the refrigerator, leftover pie will keep for about 2 days.

CANDIED SPICED PECANS

Makes 3 cups ■ **Prep Time:** 5 minutes / **Bake Time:** 10 to 15 minutes

Pecan halves are glazed in a caramelized, sugary coating to create a tempting treat for the holidays or a satisfying snack any time of year.

3 cups pecan halves

6 tablespoons maple syrup, divided

3 tablespoons vegan dark brown sugar

1 teaspoon pumpkin pie spice *or* ground cinnamon

Preheat the oven to 350°F. Line a large, rimmed baking pan with unbleached parchment paper.

Put the pecan halves, 3 tablespoons maple syrup, brown sugar, and pumpkin pie spice or ground cinnamon in a medium-sized bowl and stir with a large spoon to evenly coat the pecans.

Transfer the pecan mixture to the prepared pan and spread it in an even layer. Bake for 10 to 15 minutes, or until golden brown, checking *often* so the pecans do not burn.

Put the pan on a wire rack and let cool 15 minutes. Transfer the pecans to a medium-sized bowl and toss with the remaining 3 tablespoons maple syrup. Let cool 15 minutes more and serve, or refrigerate and serve cold. Covered tightly and stored in the refrigerator, *Candied Spiced Pecans* will keep for about 1 week.

DATE-NUT SNOWBALLS

Makes 10 large truffles or 16 small truffles ■ **Prep Time:** 25 minutes /
Refrigeration Time: 1 to 24 hours

These quick-to-prepare, pretty "snowballs" are fun to serve at holiday time. A
cross between a soft cookie and a truffle, I like to arrange them on a colorful
plate, set them in the center of the table, and watch 'em disappear!

2½ tablespoons
   unsweetened shredded
   dried coconut

2 tablespoons vegan
   confectioner's
   (powdered) sugar

½ cup pecan halves,
   roughly chopped

2 tablespoons maple syrup

12 large Medjool dates,
   pitted and chopped

⅛ rounded teaspoon
   pumpkin pie spice
   (see Chef's Note)

Line a small, rimmed baking sheet with
unbleached parchment paper. Put the coconut
and sugar in a blender and process into a fine
powder. Transfer the mixture to a small bowl and
set aside.

Put the pecans, maple syrup, dates, and
pumpkin pie spice, in the order listed, in a high-
performance blending appliance and process (by
pulsing) to the consistency of soft dough. (You
will need to stop the blending appliance once or
twice to scrape the sides down.)

Transfer the date mixture to a medium-sized
bowl. (It will be *very, very sticky!*) Spoon out
some of the date mixture, and roll it into a ball.
Continue in this manner to form 10 large or 16
small "snowballs."

Roll each "snowball" in the coconut/sugar mixture until thoroughly coated
and place it on the prepared baking sheet. Loosely cover and refrigerate for 1 to 24
hours. Stored in an airtight container in the refrigerator, "snowballs" will keep up
to 4 days.

CHEF'S NOTE

■ If desired, use *Mom's Pumpkin Pie Spice* (page 110) in this recipe.

THREE-INGREDIENT TRUFFLES

Makes 10 to 12 truffles ■ **Prep Time:** 17 minutes / **Refrigeration Time:** 1 to 24 hours

Wow! So easy, so tasty, so jazzylicious! Serve these gems for a healthy snack, weeknight dessert or festive treat.

2 tablespoons maple syrup

12 large Medjool dates, pitted and chopped

⅓ cup unsweetened shredded dried coconut

Line a small, rimmed baking sheet with unbleached parchment paper.

Put all of the ingredients, in the order listed, in a high-performance blending appliance and process (by pulsing) to the consistency of soft dough. (You will need to stop the blending appliance once or twice to scrape the sides down.)

Transfer the date mixture to a medium-sized bowl. (It will be *very, very sticky*!) Gather a heaping tablespoon of the date mixture and gently roll it into a ball, forming a truffle. Put the truffle on the prepared baking sheet.

Continue with the remaining date mixture until you have formed 10 to 12 truffles. Cover and refrigerate for 1 to 24 hours. Stored in an airtight container in the refrigerator, truffles will keep up to 4 days.

VANILLA "CREAM" DATE CARAMEL SAUCE

Makes ¾ to 1 cup ■ **Prep Time:** 10 minutes

Fresh dates blended with vegan vanilla "creamer," along with a touch of maple syrup, and plain old H₂O creates an incredibly smooth and authentic tasting "caramel" sauce to top your favorite plant-powered dessert creations!

5 tablespoons vanilla flavored dairy-free "creamer"

¼ cup water, plus more as needed

2 tablespoons maple syrup

¾ cup (firmly packed) pitted and diced Medjool dates (from 7 to 9 large dates)

Put all of the ingredients in the order listed in a blender and process until very smooth and no trace of date pieces remain.

For a thinner caramel, add more water, 1 tablespoon at a time, to achieve the desired consistency. Stored in an airtight container in the refrigerator, the sauce will keep up to 3 days.

VARIATION

■ **Vanilla-Orange "Cream" Date Caramel Sauce**: Replace the water in the recipe with ¼ cup orange juice, plus more as needed. This citrusy caramel sauce is wonderful drizzled over *Orange Creamy, Dreamy Pie with Chocolate Chip Cookie Crumb Crust* (page 248).

VEGAN TANGERINE WHIPPED CREAM TOPPING

Makes about ¾ cup ■ **Prep Time:** 10 minutes / **Refrigeration Time:** 2 hours

Tangy tangerine juice provides a powerful punch of flavor in this delectable dessert cream topping. Serve it spooned over cakes, pies, fresh fruit, or *Maple-Espresso Chocolate Mousse* (page 244).

½ cup raw cashews (soaked, drained, and rinsed, see Chef's Note)

3 to 4 ounces extra-firm regular tofu (refrigerated tub), drained and crumbled

¼ cup freshly squeezed tangerine or orange juice (see Chef's Note)

2 tablespoons maple syrup

Put the soaked and drained cashews, tofu, tangerine or orange juice, and maple syrup in a blender container. Blend for 30 seconds, or until completely smooth, adding a bit more juice (or water) if needed to achieve desired consistency. Cover and refrigerate for 2 hours, or until well chilled.

CHEF'S NOTES

■ To soak the cashews, put the raw cashews and ¼ cup water into a small bowl. Refrigerate for 1 to 4 hours. Drain the cashews and rinse thoroughly in cold water. Proceed as directed.

■ If preferred you may use bottled tangerine or orange juice in place of the freshly squeezed.

VARIATIONS

■ **Vegan Vanilla Whipped Cream Topping:** Replace the orange juice with ¼ cup sweetened vanilla-flavored dairy-free milk, plus more if needed. Proceed with recipe as directed.

■ **Vegan Lemon Cream Topping:** Replace the orange juice with 3 tablespoons freshly squeezed lemon juice, plus more if needed. Add an additional 1 tablespoon of maple syrup. Proceed with recipe as directed.

IN CONCLUSION

Folks often ask me: "Laura, what inspired *you* to focus on a purely plant-based way of living and eating?" My personal reasons for embracing a vegan diet are threefold: my compassion for animals, my desire for better health, and my aim to be more environmentally responsible.

I have a motto: "Making the world a better place, one recipe at a time." If you're new to the advantages of plant-based cooking, that may seem a bit nonsensical. How can a recipe make the world a better place? Yet when you consider the many reasons *why* people embrace a plant-based diet, such as concern for animal welfare, seeking a healthier, wholesome lifestyle, and/or being more environmentally mindful, the benefits are clear.

When contemplating transitioning to more plant-based meals, many people ask, "What will I eat if I don't eat meat, milk, cheese, or eggs?" The truth is, there are plentiful meat, egg, and dairy product substitutions widely available in most supermarkets, making it a breeze to cook tasty vegan versions of American classic recipes. Or—you may ask—"Where will I *buy* my food?" In this book, I have focused all of the recipes on ingredients that can be found in any well-stocked supermarket. Plus, I have included all of the basic information needed to start cooking delicious, easy-to-prepare, and wholesome vegan meals at home.

So, whether you are just starting on the path to adding more plant-based meals into your weekly menu plan, or you have been a dedicated vegan for many years, I hope that the recipes, ideas, and tips in this book have helped you to create easy and yummy vegan menus that your entire family will appreciate.

> Yes: we can *all* help to save the world—one recipe at a time!

Wishing you and your family good health. Be happy, be healthy, and be well!

With Gratitude, Love, and Light,

Laura

ACKNOWLEDGMENTS

THIS BOOK WAS written with the support of so many people whom I thank with all my heart!

First, infinite gratitude goes to my husband Andy, whose love and faith in me, along with his daily enthusiasm to be my Chief Recipe Tester, makes life worthwhile.

Forever thanks goes to my supportive and loving family. Your unconditional love and encouragement has meant the world to me all these years. A special thank you to my incredible mother for her constant faith in me and for sharing our treasured family recipes with me! Thank you so much to my late father and wonderful step-mom, Chris whose enthusiasm for my creative life-path has never wavered and for inspiring and supporting me to continue on this journey. Gratitude goes to my lovely mother-in-law, Anita and late father-in-law, Jack for always believing in me and generously backing me along the way. Thank you to my beautiful, talented sister Julie and awesome brother-in-law, Rob—for your on-going help, input, hard work, and support! A special thank you goes to cousin Purnima for her continued faith in helping to make this life path happen!

Thank you to my lifelong friends Debby, Sara, Lili, and Kit for continually lending an ear and sharing helpful advice, reassurance, inspiration, and love along the way!

Deep appreciation goes to the amazing Regina Eisenberg who has never wavered in her commitment to *Jazzy Vegetarian*, helping transform the television series from dream to reality. I gratefully appreciate Bob Petts, Angee Simmons and all of the fine folks at *NETA* for their excellent job in distributing the television program.

A big thank you goes to the wonderful Hatherleigh Press team of Andrew Flach, Ryan Tumambing, and Ryan Kennedy, for their kind and expert guidance, and for believing in me and this book!

A heart-filled thanks goes to my solid support group of amazing vegan authors, bloggers and health professionals: Julieanna Hever, Nava Atlas, Annie Oliverio, Rebecca Gilbert, Hannah Kaminsky, Dianne Wenz, Zel Allen, Zsu Dever, and so many more, for your continued support through the years. To the super talented Christina Pirello, for inspiring vegan eating on public television when the task seemed impossible. Look at us now! To Farm Sanctuary and the tireless leadership of Gene Baur, eternal gratitude for dedicating your lives to improve the welfare of animals.

Lastly, a big thanks to all of the wonderful fans and viewers of *Jazzy Vegetarian*, without whom I wouldn't be publishing another cookbook! Thank you for your ongoing support!

And, as always—to ALL of the animals on this Earth: This book is for *you*.

ADDITIONAL ACKNOWLEDGMENTS

Laura and Jazzy Vegetarian thanks and acknowledges our Season Nine sponsors, whose generous support has made it possible to share these recipes with the world.

Laura and Jazzy Vegetarian thankfully recognize our past sponsors: Earth Fare, Soom Foods, Bertolli, Vitamix, Tropicana, Quaker, and Pascha Chocolate.

Laura and Jazzy Vegetarian are grateful for our Season Nine brand partners who kindly helped to make this season of television achievable! A BIG thank you and deep appreciation goes to: *Electrolux Appliances, April Cornell, Worthy Flavors, Mother Earth Food, Melissa's Produce, Carpe Diem Hardware, Bob's Red Mill, Anderson's Pure Maple Syrup, Graftobian Make-Up Company, Anolon, OXO, Cardinal International, American Standard,* and *B&H Photo.* We could not have filmed this season without your substantial support!

INDEX

ABOUT THE AUTHOR

LAURA THEODORE is a nationally recognized television personality, podcast radio host, celebrity PBS vegan chef, renowned jazz singer and award-winning cookbook author. Laura is co-creator of the highly successful *Jazzy Vegetarian* cooking series on national public television and she is host of the *Jazzy Vegetarian Podcast* on Unity Online Radio.

Laura is author of six cookbooks, including: *Vegan for Everyone,* which won a bronze medal at the 2021 IPPY awards, *Laura Theodore's Vegan-Ease,* and *Deliciously Vegan*, which won silver medals at the IBPA Benjamin Franklin Awards, Midwest Book Awards and the 2019 Living Now Book Awards. Laura and *Jazzy Vegetarian* are recipients of the Taste Award for Best Health and Fitness Television Program (Food and Diet), and were inducted into the Taste Hall of Fame.

Laura has been on the cover of three prestigious magazines: *American Vegan, Jazzin',* and *La Fashionista Compassionista.* She has made guest appearances on *The Talk* on CBS, *Insider/Entertainment Tonight* and the *WCBS News Radio Health and Wellbeing Report.* She has been featured in the *New York Times, New York Daily News, Mother Earth Living, VegNews, Family Circle, Readers Digest,* and *PBS Food*, among other highly respected news, food, music, and lifestyle-related journals.

As a globally recognized award-winning jazz singer and songwriter, Laura has recorded six solo CDs, including her release with the late, great guitarist Joe Beck entitled "Golden Earrings," which was on the GRAMMY® list in the category of "Best Jazz Vocal Album." Laura has toured throughout the country, performing at numerous major events, such as Night of 100 Stars, Fire and Ice Ball, and The American Film Awards.

On the acting side of things, Laura has appeared in over sixty plays and musicals including Off-Broadway for two years in the hit show *Beehive,* which earned her a coveted Backstage Bistro Award. She was honored with the Denver Critics Drama Circle Award as "Best Actress in a Musical," for her starring role as Janis Joplin in the world premiere production of *Love, Janis.*

With her love for good food, compassion for animals, and enthusiasm for great music, multi-talented personality, Laura Theodore truly *is* the *Jazzy Vegetarian*. Learn more about Laura and Jazzy Vegetarian at: www.jazzyvegetarian.com

EASY VEGAN HOME COOKING

Library of Congress Cataloging-in-Publication Data is available upon request.

ISBN: 978-1-57826-925-9

Cover and interior design by CAROLYN KASPER

Cover, interior and food photography by LAURA THEODORE AND ANDY EBBERBACH

Fresh fruits and vegetables provided in part by WORTHY FLAVORS

Local produce provided in part by MOTHER EARTH FOOD

Specialty produce provided in part by MELISSA'S PRODUCE

Maple syrup provided by ANDERSON'S PURE MAPLE SYRUP

Laura's makeup provided in part by GRAFTOBIAN MAKE-UP COMPANY

Dinnerware provided in part by CARDINAL INTERNATIONAL

Table linens provided in part by APRIL CORNELL

Printed in the United States

10 9 8 7 6 5 4 3 2 1